Statistics for the Statistically Challenged

The Statistical Concepts You Need to Pass a Statistics Course

ANTHONY STAHELSKI

ISBN: 1463773552

ISBN-13: 9781463773557

Prologue: The Culture of Statistics

Taking an introductory statistics course is like visiting a non-English speaking country for the first time. Very few people speak or understand English, and none of the newspapers, TV shows or street signs are in English. The body language gestures that supplement the spoken language are also foreign. Nonetheless, you understand some things because some of the behaviors you see, such as smiling and frowning, are common to all humans.

Similarly, some aspects of statistics, such as bar graphs and averages, will be familiar to you from newspapers and television. These descriptive statistics are easy to understand because they simply summarize numerical information gathered from a particular sample of data with minimal use of symbols and formulas.

However, as you attempt to learn inferential statistics you may feel like you are in a foreign country. Inferential statistics are the methods for generalizing from samples to larger groups that were not sampled. Unfortunately the methods, symbols and formulas of inferential statistics are often like signposts printed in a different language. The purpose of this primer is to translate the language of inferential statistics into English to enhance your understanding of statistics at the most basic conceptual level.

My experience with struggling statistics students leads me to the conclusion that if students first learn the *concepts* that underlie the symbols and formulas, then they can actually understand the symbols and successfully manipulate the formulas. Therefore this primer thoroughly discusses, in Chapters 1 through 7, the conceptual logic underlying inferential statistics. This conceptual understanding is then applied to the translation of statistical symbols and formulas in Chapters 8 through 11.

Since the focus of the primer is on the concepts that apply to **all** inferential statistical formulas, the memorization and manipulation of specific statistical formulas are not required in this primer. The formulas in Chapters 8 through 11 are presented as examples to illuminate these common concepts, and to show you the translated versions of the most popular inferential statistics. A theme in this primer is that the conceptual similarities among statistical formulas are much more important than the differences between formulas.

The seven concepts are sequentially charted in Figure 1. When you look at this figure it is possible that the concepts will seem foreign to you. However, once the concepts are individually explained in Chapters 1 through 7 understanding the logical flow of the concepts from one to the next will be easier.

THE SEVEN CONCEPTS OF INFERENTIAL STATISTICS

CONCEPT 1 (CHAPTER 1) — ALL UNIVERSAL (POPULATION) EVENTS HAVE MULTIPLE, UNKNOWN, AND RANDOM CAUSES AND EFFECTS

CONCEPT 2 (CHAPTER 2) — EVENTS ARE NEVER OBSERVED AT THE UNIVERSAL POPULATION LEVEL, ALWAYS AT THE SAMPLE LEVEL

CONCEPT 3 (CHAPTER 3) — IF ALL EVENTS HAVE RANDOM AND MULTIPLE EFFECTS (OUTCOMES), AND IF EVENTS CAN ONLY BE STUDIED AT THE SAMPLE LEVEL, THEN THE OUTCOME OF ANY SINGLE EVENT CAN ONLY BE CONCEIVED IN TERMS OF PROBABILITIES, NOT ABSOLUTES

CONCEPT 4 (CHAPTER 4) — THE DATA AND THE DESCRIPTIVE STATISTICS DERIVED FROM THE SAMPLE ARE ASSUMED TO COME FROM RANDOM VARIABLE POPULATIONS THAT ARE THEORIZED TO HAVE EITHER PARAMETRIC OR NON PARAMETRIC DISTRIBUTIONS

CONCEPT 5 (CHAPTER 5) — IF THERE IS MORE THAN ONE POSSIBLE OUTCOME TO ANY EVENT, THEN IT IS POSSIBLE TO DIVIDE THESE POSSIBLE OUTCOMES INTO THE OUTCOME OF INTEREST (THE ALTERNATE HYPOTHESIS) AND ALL OTHER OUTCOMES (THE NULL HYPOTHESIS)

CONCEPT 6 (CHAPTER 6) — IF THE NUMBER FROM THE COMPARISON OF THE NULL AND ALTERNATIVE HYPOTHESIS IS THE SIGNAL, THEN A MEASURE OF DISPERSION IS NOISE

CONCEPT 7 (CHAPTER 7) — SINCE THE INFERENCE TEST FORMULAS USE SAMPLE DATA FOR THE ALTERNATIVE HYPOTHESIS AND FOR NOISE, THEN THE SPECIFIC CHARACTER OF EACH FORMULA CAN VARY DEPENDING ON THE MEASUREMENT COMPLEXITY OF THE SAMPLE DATA

FIGURE 1

This primer uses words and pictures to present the concepts, and spends plenty of time explaining each one before going onto the next concept. Learning the concepts is similar to learning the basic structure of a new language. Understanding the concepts will give you the mental tools necessary to understand inferential statistical language and symbols, and to properly use every statistical inference test/formula you are likely to confront.

The primer is divided into three sections. Section 1 contains seven chapters. Each of these chapters is dedicated to one of the seven concepts. Each chapter contains a chapter preview and a chapter summary. The first four chapters also contain glossaries of terms used in that chapter to help you understand the concepts as quickly as possible, the primer is purposely repetitive; at the beginning of Chapters 2 through 7 all the previously introduced concepts, with additional integrative material added, are repeated in the chapter preview after the new concept is presented.

The repetitious presentation of these concepts provides a foundation for understanding inferential statistical formulas, some of which are presented in Section 2, Chapters 8, 9 and 10. Section 3 presents a statistical decision tree in Chapter 11 that utilizes and unites the presented concepts. The primer concludes with a chapter on additional readings and exercises useful to students.

<u>The primer is intended to supplement your introductory statistics textbook</u>. You should read and re-read the primer to understand the concepts as you progress through the course, using your growing conceptual understanding to help you work with the formulas and problems presented in your text and lecture material.

Table of Contents

Section 1:

The Seven Concepts of Inferential Statistics

In Section 1, seven concepts necessary for understanding inferential statistics are presented before discussing statistical formulas in Section 2. Each chapter presents in depth one of the seven concepts. I choose the particular sequence of concept presentation, shown graphically in Figure 1, because it made the most sense to students who read earlier versions of the primer, and because there is a logical reason for this order that will become clear as you learn the concepts. However, you may find that learning the concepts in a different order improves your understanding. Or, you may find that learning a certain concept is important to you at a particular time during your statistics course, and another concept becomes important at a different time in the course.

Chapter 1:

A Set of Three Assumptions: Multiplicity, The Unknown, and Randomness

Chapter Preview

Concept 1:All population events have multiple, unknown and random causes and effects

It is assumed that all events at the universal (population) level have multiple (more than one) possible causes and effects, that these causes and effects are initially unknown, and that the causes and effects are random, unless empirically proven otherwise.

Concept 1 is composed of three assumptions about the nature of all things, i. e., the universe. Since we know so little about the universe we can only make assumptions about the characteristics of the universe. Universal events are assumed to be multiple (complex), unknown, and random for two reasons. First, scientific investigation would not be justified if other assumptions were made. Second, researchers believe that the consequences of this set of assumptions are least harmful to society.

Chapter Glossary

Cause. An event that produces an effect, result or consequence.

Multiple (Complex). Consisting of interconnected or interwoven parts; an intricate or complicated structure.

Descriptive Statistics. Numbers and/or graphs that are used to describe and summarize data.

Empirical. Data derived from naturalistic observtion or from experimental procedures.

False Negative Error. A case excluded by various criteria that is in fact qualified.

False Positive Error. The inclusion of an unqualified case because of imperfections in the selection criteria.

Inferential Statistics. The process of reaching a conclusion about unobserved events from data collected from observed events.

Random. Having no specific pattern or objective; lacking causal relationships; haphazard.

Simple. Having or composed of one thing or part only; not combined or compound.

Universe (population). An infinite or very large number of entities, events or organisms.

A. Inference: The Process of Saying Something About the Unobserved on the Basis of the Observed

The definition of inferential statistics indicates that somehow this type of statistics is used to say something about the unobserved on the basis of the observed. Researchers use inferential statistics to say something meaningful about a "universe" (a huge group of events, objects or organisms) even though this universe has not been observed (studied). An example of an organism universe that will never be observed would be all the humans that are currently alive, plus all the humans that have existed and already died, plus all the humans that will be born in the future.

However, researchers can use observed facts (descriptive statistics) gathered from a study of a small group of events, objects or organisms and make inferences about the nature of the unobserved universal group of events, objects or organisms. In inferential statistics researchers make a conclusion about a larger unknown from a smaller known. This inference process is guided by an initial set of assumptions about the nature of universes- again, huge numbers of a particular kind of event, object or organism. These "universes" are also referred to as populations. Since these populations have not been observed in their totality (nor will they ever be, as we shall see in Chapter 2) we cannot start the inferential statistics process with observed facts about these universal populations.

B. The First Assumption: Universes Are Complex (Multiple)

An event is <u>simple</u> if it has only one, or very few, causes and effects, and an event is <u>complex</u> if it has multiple causes and multiple effects. The research process starts with the assumption that a universe is complex rather than simple, that every event has multiple cause and effect connections with other events, and that this interconnectedness could extend infinitely.

However, a research study is simple. Any study can examine only a few of the infinite number of connections. If a universe was assumed to be simple, the results of a research study that looked at a few causes and effects would be all that researchers need to know about that event or entity. Investigation of that particular event could end and researchers could quickly move on to studying other events. This might be a dangerous if a universe is in fact complex because there might be other unknown variables affecting the event or entity that would cause the event or entity to act in unexpected ways at inopportune times.

C. The Second Assumption: Universes Are Unknown

Researchers first assume that a universe is infinitely complex, yet the process of research allows us to study only a few variables at a time. Therefore we will never know about all the variables possibly affecting or affected by a given event. Any study examining a given event would be like shining a flashlight in the dark; you can only see the narrow range that is illuminated by the light, the rest of your surroundings remain in darkness. The opposite assumption, that the causes and effects of an event are known, provides no justification for scientific investigation. The purpose of research is to explore the unknown. If researchers already know the complex web of cause and effect surrounding an event there is no need for research. Since the possible effects of most variables are assumed to be in the "darkness" and therefore unknown, researchers also believe that it is also better to assume that the universe is random.

D. The Third Assumption: Universes Are Random

Researchers could assume that every event in a universe is causal, and that there are no random events. Or, researchers could assume that some events are causal and some are random. Finally, researchers could assume that every event is random. The definition of random indicates that there are no causal relations in the universe if it is assumed that all events are randomly generated.

What's wrong with assuming the universe is causal? It would probably be more comforting to many of us to assume that there is causal order in a universe. However, from a research perspective, it would be difficult to assume universal causality if researchers are assuming that a universe is infinitely complex and basically unknown. The ability to empirically look for causal relations is limited to the examination of a few variables at a time. Just because researchers find a few causal relations in a few studies doesn't mean that the rest of an infinitely complex and unknown universe is causal!

E. The Three Assumptions Together

There are further problems with assuming a universe is causal, as Figure 2 on page 8 indicates. In this figure there are four possibilities, created by comparing the options on each axis. On the horizontal (X) axis a universe is actually either simple, known, and causal, or it is complex, unknown, and random. However, since a universe is unobservable by humans, we can only make assumptions about it's nature. The vertical (Y) axis indicates that we could either assume that a universe is simple, known, and causal, or that it is complex, unknown, and random. The division of each axis into two categories leads to the four cells in the chart. In two of the cells, the lower left and the upper right, there is no error because the reality and the assumption correspond. In the other two cells, the upper left and the lower right cells, the reality and the assumption do not correspond. The consequences of each of these "errors" are different. The false negative error shown in the lower right cell indicates that researchers are being too tentative- a universe is simpler and more causal than assumed. The false positive error shown in the upper left cell indicates that researchers are overstepping ourselves, by assuming simplicity and causality when none exists.

Both assumption sets can lead to possible mistakes in our thinking about a universe. Picking one assumption set possibly leads to one type of error, picking the other set possibly leads to the other error. Which type of error do scientists consider to be more harmful? To answer this question a few things need to be said about the research process. No scientist would claim that research is a foolproof process. <u>There is no such thing as a perfect study</u>. All studies have flaws; some have more, some have less. If the research process is flawed then the conclusions drawn from the results of the research might be wrong.

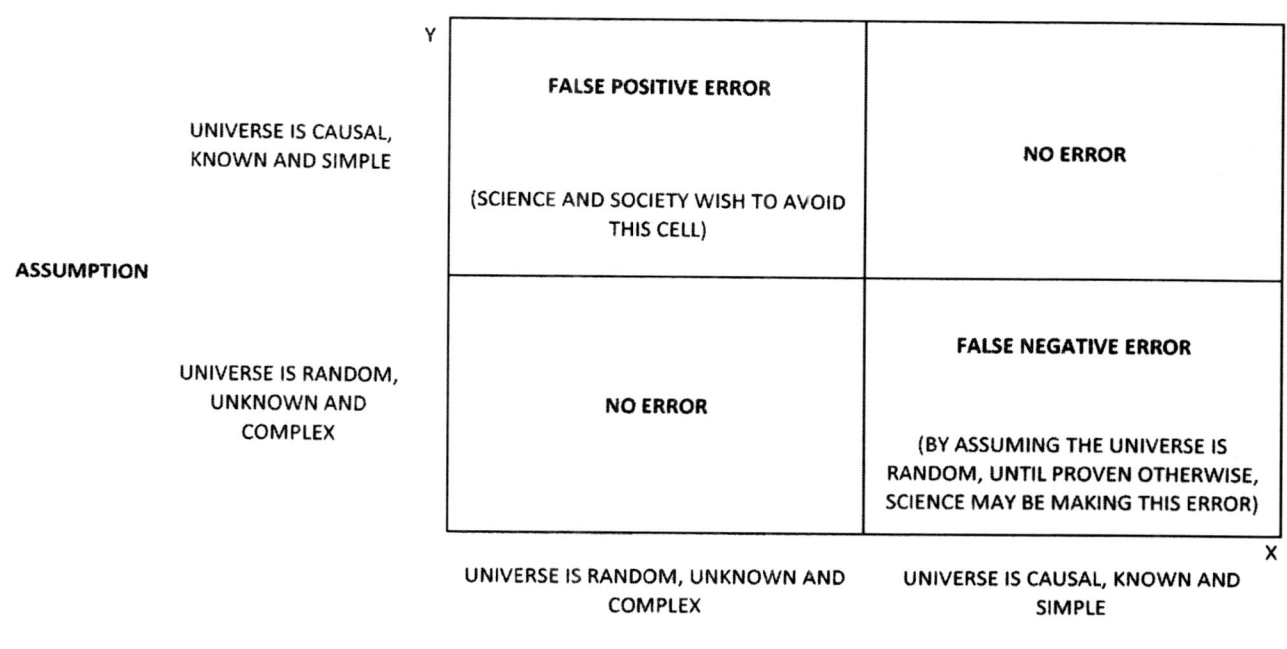

FIGURE 2

If the way that researchers gather information about the universe is imperfect and the conclusions possibly wrong, which set of assumptions should be made? If the conclusions about causality might be wrong, it makes sense to be conservative and humble, which means avoiding the false positive error, even if it means increasing the risk of making the false negative error. The false positive error consists of calling unqualified data "knowledge" on the basis of imperfect research methods.

To avoid the false positive error we postulate that every process in the universe is multiply complex, unknown, and random unless demonstrated otherwise by experiment or some other form of acceptable empirical research. This set of assumptions makes it difficult for data to ever be completely accepted by the scientific community as knowledge or truth. Scientists believe that it is possible that causal, nonrandom relations do exist in the universe, but that the existence of a few empirically proven causal relations does not constitute proof that the entire universe is causal. In spite of the ever-growing empirical evidence of causality in the universe, scientists still assume that the universe is random until empirically demonstrated otherwise, for fear that the scientific community, and humanity in general, will falsely accept causal relations where none exist. Scientists believe the dangers inherent in basing social policy decisions on an unproven causal relation outweigh the consequences of rejecting an actual causal relation. The release of inadequately studied drugs, such as thalidomide, for public consumption is a tragic example of the false positive error in action.

Chapter Summary

All the knowledge that has been gathered over the last 5000 years since the advent of literacy is a very small portion of the total possible knowledge of any universe. Since so little is actually known, the process of inferential statistics starts with assumptions rather than facts. We choose to start with assumptions- the universe is infinitely complex, unknown and random- that essentially indicate the strong possibility that any part of our accumulated or future knowledge could be wrong. Given how frequently we humans have been wrong in our search for universal truth, this set of assumptions seems to be a safer starting point than the opposite set of assumptions.

Chapter 2:

Finite Samples and Infinite Populations

Chapter Preview

Concept 2: Events are never observed at the universal (population) level, always at the sample level.

Therefore, to empirically prove causal relations at the universal level, we must infer from a sample of event or entity observations to the total population of potential event or entity observations.

Concept 1 assumed that all events at a universal (population) level are complex (have more than one possible cause and effect), that these causes and effects are unknown, and that the causes and effects are random, unless empirically proven otherwise.

We start with assumptions about the nature of the universe because events at the universal (population) level can never be observed. Instead, we observe portions of events called samples. Therefore, to empirically prove causal relations at the universal level, we infer from a sample of observations to the total population of potential observations.

The assumption set that composes Concept 1 refers to events or entities at a population level. A "population level" means all the events or entities: the total universe of occurrences of a particular event, or the total universe of objects or organisms. If researchers want to discover the universal nature of an event or entity, they must somehow take into consideration the total population of occurrences. However, as was discussed in Section A of the last chapter, it is never possible to study the total population of occurrences of any event, object or organism. Researchers can only study portions of populations called samples. This chapter discusses how it is possible to make statements about populations even though populations are never studied.

Chapter Glossary

Deductive Logic. The process of reasoning from formal premises or propositions (the general) to a conclusion (the particular).

Inductive Logic. The process by which inference is made from observed sample data (the particular) to an unobserved population (the general).

Observation. The act of paying attention or noticing.

Population (Universe). The larger set of events, objects or organisms from which a sample is taken.

Random Selection. The process of selecting a sample from a population in a way that results in every member of the population having an equal chance of being in the sample.

Research. Scholarly investigation or inquiry.

Sample. Portion, piece, or segment regarded as representative of a whole; or, an entity or specimen representative of a class; or, more specifically statistical, a set of elements drawn from and analyzed to estimate the characteristics of a population.

Statistical Inference Tests. The numerical formulas that test whether descriptive statistics generated from sample data represent the population.

A. The Population Level, the Sample Level and Randomness.

In spite of assuming that universes are complex, unknown and random, researchers ultimately want to discover general causal principles that apply at universal (population) levels. Research findings about humans cannot become general principles if they only apply to a sample of one individual or to a very small group of individuals. However, one of the limitations of the research process is that data are gathered from single individuals and small groups called samples, not larger groups called populations. How are samples and populations related?

As the glossary definition indicates, a universe can be characterized as a populations of events, objects or organisms. An event population might be something as simple as tooth-brushing, an event that happens billions of times a day around the world. An object population could be all the automobiles ever made, and an organism population could be the current world human population. Since we do not have the time, energy or resources to study populations, data on any event, object or organism are collected from portions of populations called samples.

Again as the glossary indicates, a sample is a "portion, piece or segment regarded as representative of a whole"; more specifically statistical, "a set of elements drawn from and analyzed to estimate the characteristics of a population." According to the above definitions, samples are drawn from populations. Once a sample is drawn, data are collected from that sample. The data are often used to prove or disprove the existence of population (universal) causal relations. Given this use of sample data, samples should fairly represent the variability in the populations. Random sample selection is frequently the best way to assure that a sample fairly represents the population distribution. However, a random process does not produce the same outcome or consequence every time it occurs under identical circumstances. Although, samples can be taken from a population under approximately identical circumstances each time a sample is taken, this definition indicates that randomly drawing different samples from a population will not result in identical samples being drawn each time. Since no two events, objects or organisms are ever exactly alike (no two tooth-brushings, cars or individuals are ever exactly alike), there is always variation in the composition of a population, and therefore in any samples drawn from a population. Nonetheless, despite variability in the random sampling process, the use of randomness is still the best way to assure samples that are reasonably representative samples of the population.

B. A step by step approach of relating a sample to a population

Figure 3 diagrammatically shows the steps taken to define the relation between a sample and a population. In Step 1, which occurs before collecting sample data, the population is first defined: Is it all of humanity? all females? all males? all Americans? all college students? A sample cannot be defined or selected without first defining the population.

Step 2, defining the sample, also occurs before any data are collected. The population definition limits the sample definition possibilities. If the population is defined as females, obviously any samples from that population will contain only females. However, within the limits imposed by the population definition the sample could come from all portions of the population, or from a particular portion. For example, the sample could be composed only of females 30 to 40 years of age or it could be composed of females from all age groups.

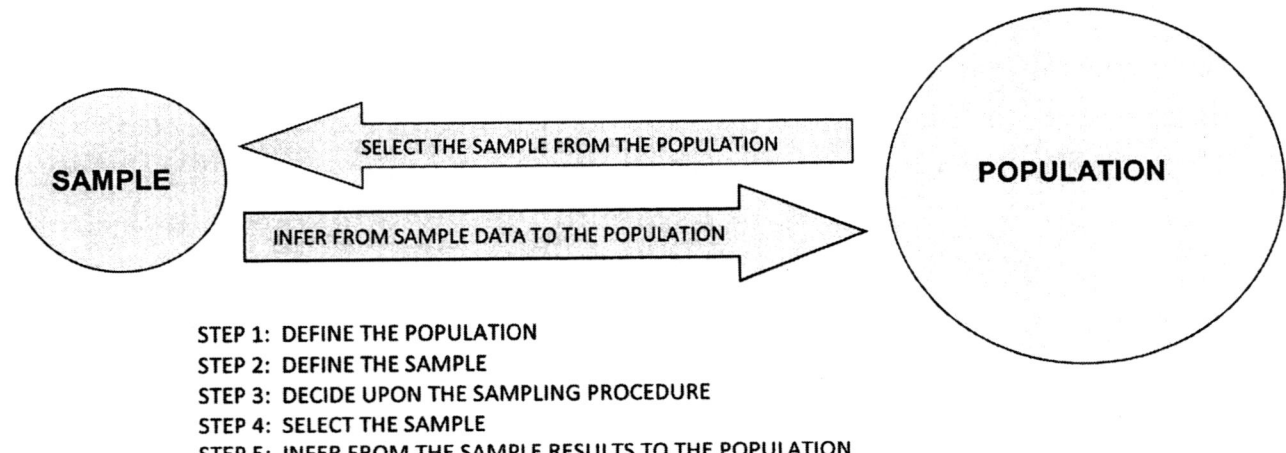

STEP 1: DEFINE THE POPULATION
STEP 2: DEFINE THE SAMPLE
STEP 3: DECIDE UPON THE SAMPLING PROCEDURE
STEP 4: SELECT THE SAMPLE
STEP 5: INFER FROM THE SAMPLE RESULTS TO THE POPULATION

FIGURE 3

Once the sample is defined a sampling procedure is decided upon in Step 3. The particular sampling procedure helps to answer the following question: "Has the sample been representatively selected from the population?" A fair, representative sample is achieved if each member of the defined population has an equal chance (with every other member) of being in the sample. Some procedures used to provide equal opportunity use randomness as the basis of selection.

In step 4 the sample is selected and data are collected from that sample. Since the data collected in Step 4 are not collected on every member of a population, then we need to infer from the sample data to the population, as indicated in Step 5. A statistical inference involves reaching a conclusion about a population based on evidence taken only from data collected from a sample of that population.

Randomness can play a part in the sample to population inference process. Why is randomness important in reaching conclusions about a population from evidence gathered from a sample? This question can be answered by discussing individual differences.

C. The effects of individual differences on samples and populations

Differences exist between individuals in all the basic dimensions (physical, intellectual, emotional, psychological) and in all the variables associated with these dimensions. Most of these variables will not be explicitly examined in any given study, and therefore the potential effects of these variables on the studied event, object or organism are unknown and presumed to be random.

Individual differences (variability both within and across individuals) are the reason that we sample more than one individual in any study. <u>If there were no individual differences we would need to collect data on only one individual to find out about the defined population.</u> Since any given individual would give exactly the same insights into human nature and behavior as any other individual, there would be no need to be concerned about the representativeness of the selection process.

Random selection in sampling reduces the impact of individual differences. For example, if you want to measure the effects of massed practice versus intermittent practice on a rote memory task, individuals of high and low intelligence should have an equal chance of being in either treatment condition. Or, if you survey opinions on nuclear power, you would want to survey equally across the entire range of opinions on nuclear power. In both examples random selection from the defined population would help give representative samples.

The safest assumption to make about individual differences is that they always exist. Individual differences on all variables mean that there is a distribution of values for all variables. Since this distribution exists on every variable at the population level, a representative sampling procedure should lead to a sample that matches the population distribution. Using randomness in the sample selection process gives a reasonable opportunity to match the sample and population distributions.

Thus far populations and samples have been discussed as populations and samples of events, objects or organisms. It is now time to expand our definitions of these terms. Research is the process of observing individuals and observing the occurrences of events. For the terms "population" and "sample" to be useful in research, they need to be defined not just as individuals or events, but as <u>observations</u> on individuals and <u>occurrences</u> of events.

D. Deductive and inductive logic and expanded definitions of populations and samples

So far I have been using the term population as if it were a finite amount of individuals, and a sample as if it were some finite portion of this finite population. The use of inductive logic in research, discussed in this section, requires that the definitions of population and sample be expanded.

It is often mistakenly assumed that research is an exercise in deductive logic. While this may be true when generating hypotheses, inductive logic is used at the empirical data collection level. What are the similarities and differences between these two forms of reasoning?

Both forms of logic are used to reach conclusions. In deductive logic the conclusion can be proven to be absolutely true or false. As Figure 4 demonstrates, the deductive logic process starts with a premise, works through additional logically connected premises and deduces one of only two possible conclusions; either a true conclusion, represented by the number 1, or a false conclusion, represented by the number 0, of the set of premises. However, the premises and conclusions of deductive logic are elements of a theoretical system that are always conceptual; they are not based on observations of the world.

DEDUCTIVE LOGIC LEADS TO CERTAINTY	INDUCTIVE LOGIC LEADS TO UNCERTAINTY	DEDUCTIVE LOGIC LEADS TO CERTAINTY
PREMISE OR PREMISES LEADING TO	OBSERVATIONS LEADING TO	PREMISE OR PREMISES LEADING TO
A CONCLUSION WHICH IS ABSOLUTELY TRUE	AT LEAST TWO PROBABLE CONCLUSIONS	A CONCLUSION WHICH IS ABSOLUTELY FALSE
REPRESENTED BY THE NUMBER :	REPRESENTED BY A NUMBER BETWEEN:	REPRESENTED BY THE NUMBER:
1	0 AND 1	0
ONLY ONE POSSIBLE OUTCOME	MORE THAN ONE POSSIBLE OUTCOME	ONLY ONE POSSIBLE OUTCOME

FIGURE 4

Inductive logic is not conceptual and does not start with premises. This form of reasoning starts with observations of the world and attempts to derive a conclusion from these observations. However, this conclusion cannot be stated in absolute, true or false, terms. We can never be sure that one has observed all the specific events in existence that led to the conclusion. There is always another potential observation that could change the conclusion. Since scientific knowledge is based on inductive conclusions reached through observation, there are no absolutes in science! If there are no absolutes there are only uncertain possibilities. These possibilities are measured by probabilities, which are represented by fractions between 0 and 1.

Here is an example of observation and inductive logic in action. You are offered a lifetime job at a fabulous salary. The job is to spend the rest of your working life in a pool hall of your choice. The specific task is to observe and chart what happens to an eight ball every time it is hit by a cue ball. In the course of a lifetime, hundreds of thousands, if not millions, of observations of this event could be accumulated. Each of these observations would indicate that when the cue ball hits the eight ball with enough force, the eight ball always moves away from the cue ball. Given the vast amount of data, we can absolutely conclude that a cue ball hitting an eight ball with enough force always makes the eight ball move away from the cue ball, right? The answer is <u>no</u>. In spite of the massive number of observations, they are nevertheless a limited sample of the total number of cue ball-eight ball events occurring in the world. And, even if you somehow managed to cover all the cue-eight ball events occurring in the world during your working life, what about all the cue-eight ball events that occurred before your observations began, or that will occur after your observations are over? It could be that in an unobserved cue-eight ball event, an eight ball (not sitting flush against the cushion) moved toward the cue ball after being hit by the cue ball!

This example indicates that <u>every</u> research study (data collected from a set of observations) is based on <u>sampling</u> from the total population of observations potentially available. The example used expanded definitions of population and sample. *A population is not just the total number of events, objects or organisms, it is the total possible number of* <u>*observations*</u> *of those things, individuals or events. Similarly, a sample is not just a portion of the total number of individuals, it is the number of observations on that portion.*

The issue of sample-to-population inference is never a problem in deductive logic. Since deduction is conceptual <u>both</u> the premise and the conclusion can theoretically relate to a sample, or to an entire population. However, as the above example shows, the induction process is <u>always</u> an inference from a sample (your observations) to a population (your conclusion applied to those you did not sample and all those observations you did not make). Data collection, the induction process in action, <u>never</u> takes place at the population level, if the population is defined infinitely as all possible observations. Even if the population is more narrowly defined as a limited set of observations on a set number of individuals, data collection almost never occurs at the population level.

E. Is there such a thing as a population?

What about the United States Census? Isn't the Census a study of a population? Yes and no. Theoretically yes, in the sense that the Census is an <u>attempt</u> to gather basic numerical information about every individual in the United States once a decade. However practically the answer is no, because this attempt always fails. It fails as a population study in several ways. First, the Census data collection procedure allows certain individuals to give information about other individuals. Adults give information about children and the impaired elderly. Heads of households (or whoever fills out the forms) give information about everyone else in the household. Nothing prevents these representing individuals from exaggerating or even blatantly lying on the forms. Secondly, the Census does not gather information about every individual in the United States. What about the homeless or those who constantly change addresses? In fact, under-counting has led to complaints that many localities, especially big cities, have about the Census. Thirdly, and perhaps most importantly given our expanded definition of population, the Census is a periodic snapshot in time. The Census is not an ongoing continuous study. Immediately after the counts and information are given in a specific location circumstances could change drastically. <u>The most famous "population" study in the country is in fact a sample study</u>. Granted, the Census is based on a huge sample, but it is still not a population.

However, a few population studies, in the sense of limited observations on a very limited set of individuals, do exist. Before California Condors began to be released into the wild in the late 1990s, investigations of the Condor were population studies because the few remaining Condors were all in captivity. However, in the sense of the expanded definition of population given above, studies of the captive Condors were not population studies. What about all those Condors through history that lived and died before the captive group was studied? What about the Condors yet to be born? And, even though the total captive population was studied, the <u>observations</u> on that population were still a limited set (a sample) of the total number of potential observations on the captive Condor population.

So, do populations exist? Yes, they do, but we cannot access them! From the realistic perspective of actual data collection on limited samples, populations are infinite, universal concepts. No research study has ever been done on a population, in the expanded sense of the term. If populations cannot ever be actually studied, why is it important to relate sample results to a population?

An analogy might help to answer this question. Much of the behavior of humans is channeled toward the attainment of goals. A goal is an image, an ideal, a theoretical concept that one strives toward. However, most of us come to realize that no ideal, no goal, is ever attained perfectly. Nonetheless, just because the actual attainment of a goal never matches the ideal of the goal does not mean that goals are useless. Goals continue to be useful motivational devices. Goals are analogous to populations; behaviors toward goals are analogous to samples. We compare our actual goal attainment to our goal ideal to see how much we have accomplished. The end result of the inference process from sample data to the population also tells us how much we have accomplished because we know how likely it is that our sample data represents the population.

F. Matching the Population and the Sample Distribution.

Will the sample distribution (the sample variability) ever perfectly match the population distribution (the population variability)? Very Unlikely. Even with random sampling, there is always the possibility that the sample drawn will be different, sometimes very different, from the population. _Randomness in sampling merely reduces the chances of a serious sample-to-population inference error; it does not totally eliminate the possibility of error_. You could be unfortunate enough to randomly draw a sample from an extreme portion of the population, and therefore the sample would not fairly represent the population. Thus it is necessary to engage in the statistical inference process. _Statistical inference tests lead to an estimate of the liklihood that the sample distribution was not a good match of the population distribution. This is the sole purpose of all the inference tests you are exposed to in a statistics course!_ Without statistical inference there is no way of knowing how well the sample matches the population. Chapter 3 presents another concept, probability, that explains how this likelihood is estimated.

Chapter Summary

Concept 2 defines the universal (population) level referred to in Concept 1 as infinite populations. An infinite population is all the possible past, present and future events, objects or organisms. An infinite population can never be studied. A sample is a finite portion of an infinite population that can be studied. The data gathered from a sample are used to infer characteristics about the population, and this inference process must be conceptualized in terms of probabilities, not absolutes.

Chapter 3:

Probability Underlies the Inference Process from Samples to Populations

<u>Chapter Outline</u>

Chapter Preview
Review of Concepts 1 and 2
Concept 3
Chapter Glossary

    A. Probability, Randomness and Human Decision Making
    B. Randomness and Probability
    C. Probability Defined in Terms of the Predicted Causes of the Event of Interest
    D. Probability Defined in Terms of Random "Causes" of the Event of Interest
    E. Statistical Significance

<u>Chapter Summary</u>

Chapter Preview

Review of Concepts 1 and 2

In Concept 1 it is assumed that all events at universal (population) levels have more than one possible cause and effect, that these causes and effects are unknown, and that the causes and effects are random, unless empirically proven otherwise. Concept 2 indicates that these events are never observed at population levels, only at sample levels. Therefore, to empirically prove causal relations at population levels, researchers infer from a sample of observations to the total population of potential observations.

Concept 3: If all events have random and multiple effects (outcomes) at the population level, and if events can only be studied at the sample level, then the outcome of any single event can only be conceived in terms of probabilities, not absolutes.

Probability is a difficult concept to grasp because humans engage in categorical decision making, and because we don't often admit that randomness has an impact on our lives. A short discussion of decision making will help introduce probability and probabilistic thinking. Once probability is understood, it is easier to grasp that the sample to population inference process is always probabilistic, and that samples are never completely representative of the population they are drawn from.

Chapter Glossary

Absolute. Unlimited by restrictions or exceptions; unconditional: or, unqualified in extent or degree; total.

Probability. The degree to which it is likely that an event will occur in a certain way as opposed to other possible ways.

Statistically Significant. The degree to which an obtained value will not occur by chance (random factors) and therefore can be attributed to another (nonrandom) factor.

A. Probability, randomness and human decision making

Humans often deny that chance plays a part in their lives. We act as if we control our behavior in a variety of situations, when numerous experiments suggest that our behavior is frequently controlled by random cues present in our current situation. Observers of accidents and other negative events will often assign responsibility for the events to the victims, as a means of denying the random possibility that such events could happen to themselves.

Not only do we want to be in control by denying randomness, but we seem to want our decisions to be absolute. For example, when we see an individual who partially fits into a particular group, we will perceive that individual as having all the characteristics that we attribute to members of that group. When we identify with a sports team we tend to see "our" team as wonderfully positive and the other teams as despicably negative.

We appear to believe not only that all events have nonrandom causes and effects, but that events have only one possible cause and only one possible outcome (absolutes). The concept of probability causes us to question the usefulness of our beliefs in control and absolutes. Conceiving of events in terms of probability means thinking that there is more than one possible cause or effect for any event. Probabilistic thinking is based on the Concept 1 assumption of multiplicity in causes and effects that was discussed in Chapter 1.

This contradiction between our beliefs and the conceptual basis of probability accounts for much of our difficulty in understanding probability. Understanding probability is essential because an understanding of probability is the key to understanding inferential statistics.

B. Randomness and Probability

Given that data collection is always a sampling process based on observation and the use of inductive logic, the inference from the sample data collected to the population is always probabilistic, never absolute. Why? Another definition of the term random is: "of or designating a phenomenon that does not produce the same outcome or consequence every time it occurs under identical circumstances", helps to answer this question. Sampling from a population can be done close to identically every time sampling is done, in certain circumstances. However, just because the procedure can be done the same way each time does not mean that the <u>result</u> of the procedure is the same each time. Each sample taken from a population will most likely be at least slightly different from all other samples taken from that population. Before sampling one can never be sure of the exact characteristics of that sample. Most samples will be more or less reasonable approximations of the population distribution. However, it is always possible that a researcher has been unfortunate enough to have picked a skewed sample that is not at all representative of the population. Researchers can never be absolutely sure that the sample does fairly represent the population. Researchers can estimate the likelihood of getting samples that are more or less representative of the population. These estimates, or probabilities, are expressed as fractions.

Coin tossing is an example of the relation between samples, populations, randomness, and probabilities. This is a very simple event with only two possible outcomes, heads or tails. Each coin toss is a single sample of the universal population of coin tosses. Before any given coin toss of a fair coin it is not known whether that particular toss will yield a head or a tail. "Randomness" is composed of the effects of an infinite number of variables, which may be truly random or unknown causal. The outcome of a coin toss could be determined by the exact position of the coin in the hand, the amount of force put into the toss, the height of the toss, the number of times the coin turns in the air, the density, humidity, and velocity of the air, and so on. None of the variables mentioned (or unmentioned) are usually measured when one tosses a coin. Since none of these variables are measured the possible causes of the outcome are unknown, and the actual outcome of the toss will be determined by some random and unknown confluence of these many variables. The outcome of the sample event is unknown before it occurs and can only be conceived of in terms of what might happen within a range of possibilities; the probability associated with each possible outcome.

C. Probability Defined in Terms of the Predicted Cause of the Event of Interest

Absolutes are numerically defined as 0 and 1. Consequently the probabilities, which are not absolutes, associated with possible outcomes can be any fractional value between 0 and 1. The probability of a particular event of interest is defined as the number of particular event outcomes, such as the number of heads, divided by the total number of possible outcomes, such as the number of heads and tails:

the number of particular event outcomes

total number of possible outcomes

For a researcher, the "particular event of interest" is usually associated with what the researcher believes is the particular cause which leads to the particular event outcome. What is the probability that the effect, the event of interest, is the cause? However, the probabilities that are the ultimate results of the use of inference test formulas are **not** associated with the researcher's predicted cause! Unfortunately from the viewpoint of student understanding, the probabilities resulting from inference test formula use are associated with random "causes" that researchers have no interest in!

D. Probability Defined in terms of Random "Causes" of the Event of Interest

How does the probability formula shown above relate to the probability statements that can be seen in the tables in the back of statistics textbooks, and that you might see in research articles in journals? In the above formula the "particular event outcome" is the effect of a presumably nonrandom cause of interest to a researcher; all other possible causes are not of interest. Somewhat illogically and potentially confusing for students, probability statements used in books and journals are not based on this formula. They are based on an alternative formula that focuses on the occurrence of <u>random causes</u> (that are not of interest to a researcher) that lead to random event outcomes. This probability statement formula looks like this:

<u>the number of random event outcomes</u>

total number of possible outcomes

As an example, a research study utilizes a particular inference test formula to infer from sample data to the population. The data analysis results in the following probability statement: p. <.05. In this statement p. is an abbreviation for probability and .05=5/100. Five is the number of random event outcomes, and 100 is all possible outcomes. <u>Students frequently don't understand probability values in statistics tables and journal articles because these probability values do not represent the event (the cause and effect relation) of interest to a researcher!</u> They represent the opposite, the "leftovers" assigned to chance!

To help understand how weird this practice is, I will create the probability statement in terms of the nonrandom event of interest. The logic of the first formula and definition of probability fits better here: p.>.95, which equals 95/100, where 95 is the event of interest, and 100 is all possible events. It appears that non-randomness (the event of interest) determines the event 95 out of 100 times. A statistical table probability statement of .99 should mean that non-randomness determines the event 99 out of 100 times, and a table probability statement of .999 indicates that non-randomness determines the event 999 out of 1000 times.

Why don't researchers use probability statements that give the probability of the event of interest, as I just did? There are some good reasons why the focus of probability statements is on random events rather than the event of interest, and these reasons will be explained when the null and alternative hypothesis concepts are introduced in the next chapter.

Can the probability assigned to randomly generated outcomes ever be reduced to zero? No; regardless of how strong the evidence is that the event of interest was caused by a nonrandom cause, there is <u>always</u> the possibility (probability) of another, presumably random, factor relating to the outcome. The probability of a random "cause" can never be reduced to zero; if it could it would be an absolute, which is not possible in the inductive logic process, where data are collected from samples (and the last chapter demonstrated that all data are collected from samples). If the influence of randomness can never be reduced to zero, when is the probability of the randomness factor considered low enough so that we can be reasonably sure that a nonrandom factor caused the event of interest?

E Statistical Significance

Researchers decide arbitrarily what probability assigned to randomness (chance) is low enough to be acceptable, or, in the language of statistics, statistically significant. <u>Statistically significant</u> inference test formula results are sample data results that occurred because the possibility of chance as a determining factor is very low. We accept as statistically significant those results which have a .05, .01, or .001 probability of occurring by chance. The specific probability used to arbitrarily separate significant from non-significant results, called the alpha level, depends upon how willing a researcher is to make the wrong inference from the sample data to the population. A .05 alpha level means that, if the same type of sample were drawn from the population an infinite number of times, and the data analysis based on the sample led to the same results each time, only 5 out of every 100 times would those results have been determined by chance. If your findings result in a .05 significance level, you know that the results were unlikely to have occurred by chance. Although the results of your particular study could be one of those 5 out of every 100, you are taking a small risk in assuming that they are not.

What does a .01 alpha level mean? It is a more conservative rule. It means that results cannot be accepted as being statistically significant ("true") unless the possibility that chance determined the results is less than 1 out of 100. The .001 alpha level is even more conservative. This means that results are not statistically significant unless the possibility of chance as the determinant is less than 1 out of 1000.

Chapter Summary

If we assume that the possible causes of a single event at the population level are multiple, mostly unknown and seemingly random, then it makes sense to also assume that the possible causes of that event can only be conceptualized as probabilities, not absolutes. The use of probabilities as the ultimate result of the statistical inference process means that there is always uncertainly when inferring from sample data to populations. More broadly, it means that there is always uncertainty about the conclusions reached in scientific research. Any accepted scientific "facts" can be overthrown and replaced by new findings based on newer, and presumably better, research studies.

With a single event influenced by random factors, such as a single coin toss, it is not possible to predict any patterns or trends. However, if randomly generated events are repeated many times, characteristic patterns emerge in the distribution of outcomes to those events. How is it possible that randomness can lead to patterns? This question, which leads to Concept 4, will be answered in Chapter 4.

Chapter 4:

Patterned Randomness: Normal and Non-normal Distributions

<u>Chapter Outline</u>

Chapter Preview
Review
Concept 4

<u>Chapter Glossary</u>

   A. Distributions and Misconceptions
   B. Distributions: Parametric and Nonparametric
   C. Probability, Randomness, Distributions, and Statistical Inference Tables
   D. The Binomial Event and Distribution
   E. The Bell Shaped Normal Curve of a Parametric Distribution

<u>Chapter Summary</u>

Chapter Preview

Review

Concept 1 is a set of assumptions that all events at the universal (population) have more than one possible cause and effect, that most of these causes and effects are unknown, and that the causes and effects are random, unless empirically proven otherwise. Concept 2 states that events are never observed at the universal (population) level, always at the sample level. Therefore, to empirically prove causal relations at the universal level, we must infer from a sample of observations of events to the population of potential observations. And Concept 3 indicates that if all events have random and multiple effects, at either the sample or population levels, then the outcome of any single unobserved event can only be conceived in terms of probabilities, not absolutes.

Concept 4: The data and the descriptive statistics derived from the sample are assumed to come from random variable (event, object or organism) populations that are theorized to have either parametric or nonparametric distributions.

Concept 4 qualifies and more fully specifies the set of assumptions that make up Concept 1. Concept 4 tells us that the random variation in population values leads to characteristic patterns, known as <u>distributions</u>. If events, objects and organisms at the population level have these characteristic distributions, then presumably they are neither completely random (e.g., without pattern), completely unknown nor infinitely complex.

If Concept 4 is a correction of Concept 1, why not just start with 4? Because it is possible that the deductive logic and the empirical testing that led to acceptance of the idea of patterned distributions of population variables could be wrong. If there is at least a slim possibility that the distribution concept is wrong, then it is best to start each research project with Concept 1, that the population characteristics of the variable studied are completely unknown, infinitely complex, and "truly" (without pattern) random.

Concept 4 is important because its qualifications are incorporated into the six step statistical processing model (presented in Chapter 8). This model starts with the comparison of the null and alternative hypotheses (discussed in the next chapter) that occurs during inferential data analysis. When the inference test formula number is compared to the appropriate number from a statistical table, the comparison is done according to Concept 4, because the tables are constructed according to the distribution characteristics discussed in this chapter.

Population distributions are usually grouped into two categories, parametric (normal) and nonparametric (non-normal). Many students initially think the parametric assumptions of the normal distribution apply to all inference tests. In fact the normal distribution theoretically applies only to inference tests based on continuous, quantitative (parametric) data.

This chapter will first define and then distinguish between parametric and nonparametric distributions. Then, as an example of how a repeated randomly generated event can lead to a characteristic pattern, the nonparametric binomial distribution will be discussed. This discussion of the binomial distribution serves as a lead-in to the final portion of the chapter, the presentation of the normal distribution, a parametric distribution which maps events that are continuous and non-discrete.

Chapter Glossary

Binomial distribution. The distribution of scores (values) that results from repeating an event that has only two possible outcomes.

Continuum. A variable, graph or curve without discrete gaps between points.

Discrete (discontinuous) measures. Lacking continuity, characterized by gaps or breaks; pertaining to measures that do not form a continuum of infinitely small steps but represent instead whole numbers.

Distribution. A characteristic pattern that occurs with the repetition of a randomly generated event, which can be demonstrated by a table or graph comparing the numerical values (scores) of an event, plotted on the horizontal axis, to the frequency of the scores, plotted on the vertical axis.

Normal distribution. A distribution that does not differ significantly from the bell-shaped or Gaussian curve; in which the scores group around the mean, with the greatest number of scores near the mean and with the frequency of scores trailing off on either side of the mean.

Nonparametric. Statistical inference techniques that are based on assuming that the population is not normal, and that the event, object or organism is discrete, not continuous.

Parametric. Statistical inference techniques that are based on a set of assumptions about the population, that the event, object or organism is continuous, and that the distribution of scores from the event is normal.

Quality. A difference in kind not degree.

Quantity. Measured variation by degree not kind.

A. Distributions and Misconceptions

What is a distribution? A <u>distribution</u> is a characteristic pattern that occurs with repetitions of a randomly generated event. The outcome of any single event may be randomly generated; however, the accumulation of many repetitions of the event has a characteristic pattern called a distribution.

As stated in the Chapter Preview, population distributions are classified into two types, parametric and non-parametric. All inferential statistical tests are formulated in the context of sample data collected from a population with an assumed parametric or nonparametric distribution.

The way in which the terms parametric and nonparametric are used in statistics is confusing. In statistics a <u>parameter</u> is a characteristic of a population. If a mean and standard deviation were to be derived from a population they would be parameters of that population. Similarly, the characteristic shape of the distribution of observed values in an event, object or organism population is a parameter of that population. Given these examples of the use of the term parameter, presumably the term "non-parametric" would refer to something that is <u>not</u> a parameter. However, this is not how the term non-parametric is used in statistics!

Due to the confusing use of these two terms, students often think that parametric populations have parameters and that non-parametric populations do not have parameters. A related misconception is that parametric means that one can infer from a sample to a population, and that nonparametric means that one cannot infer from a sample to a population.

<u>These misconceptions are both incorrect</u>. All populations, both parametric and non-parametric, have parameters. And, one infers from a sample to a population with any inference test, regardless of whether the test is based on the assumption of either a normal (parametric) or non-normal (non-parametric) population distribution.

Parametric inference tests based on assumptions of normal distributions are often referred to as "distribution" statistics, and non-parametric inference tests based on non-normal distribution assumptions are often called "distribution-free" statistics. This terminology is also confusing, because it also leads to the mistaken impression that non-parametric variables do not have underlying theoretical distributions. Non-parametric variables at the population level <u>do</u> have assumed underlying distributions; it's just that these distributions are not normal. The terms "distribution" and "distribution-free" are more accurately stated as "normal distribution" and "normal distribution-free".

B. Distributions: Parametric and Nonparametric

So what exactly are parametric and nonparametric distributions? These two types of distributions come from two very different types of variables. Parametric distributions are based on continuous variables, and nonparametric distributions are based on discrete variables.

The values from parametric, continuous variables can be placed on continuums. A continuous variable value on a continuum can only be distinguished from another value arbitrarily. For example, time is a continuous variable, measured on a continuum. Time can be flexibly and infinitely divided into any sized category unit. Time could be measured anywhere from a millionth of a second (or infinitely smaller) to geological eras (or infinitely bigger). Given this infinite divisibility, category boundaries on continuous variables are arbitrary. Differences in categories along the continuum of time are quantitative differences of amount, not qualitative differences indicating the presence or absence of time. Therefore parametric events and entities are continuous (non-discrete) variables, and are considered to be quantitative (more or less) rather than qualitative (either/or), and arbitrarily categorical rather than truly categorical.

Nonparametric variables are discrete (discontinuous; not divisible). The categories that are made from a discrete variable cannot be infinitely divided into smaller and smaller or larger and larger categories. Discrete variables have a finite number of distinct and separate categories that are not arbitrary. This is because each category made from a discrete variable represents a qualitative, not a quantitative, distinction. Qualitative distinctions are differences in kind, not degree or amount. A qualitative distinction indicates the complete presence or absence of a characteristic. Membership in one category precludes membership in another category. For example, if an animal is biologically classified as a mammal it cannot be classified as a reptile.

C. Probability, Randomness, Distributions, and Statistical Inference Tables

The back of your statistics textbook contains statistical tables. The formatting and the numbers in these tables are identical to those found in any other statistics textbook. Researchers use these tables to decide whether study results from sample data have achieved a probability which is statistically significant. The inference process from samples to populations cannot be concluded without reference to these tables. Why are these tables so important, and how are they constructed?

<u>All statistical tables are constructed on the basis of randomness</u>. A third definition of random is, "of or designating an event having a relative frequency of occurrence that approaches a stable limit as the number of observations of the event increases to infinity." This definition implies that, amazingly enough, there are patterns that can be discerned in random events.

Doesn't the word pattern imply nonrandom causality? For a random event, like a fair coin toss, the outcome of any <u>single</u> event is indeed unknown before it happens. However, if one were to toss a coin over and over again, a pattern of outcomes occurs that is based on the probabilities associated with each outcome. This probability based pattern forms an outcome frequency distribution that can be graphed and tabled.

All the statistical tables that you find in the back of an introductory text are built on the probability patterns associated with the randomness of a given single event. More specifically, all tables are built upon assumed distributions that underlie random variables. How can something as orderly as a statistical table be built on randomness?

D. The binomial event and distribution

A statistical table can be built from the pattern formed by repeating a random event, the coin toss. The coin toss event is classified as a binomial (only two possible outcomes) event. The binomial event is based on sample data that is qualitative, non-continuous and categorical, and therefore nonparametric. The binomial distribution is a nonparametric distribution which is assumed to underlie binomial events. If we toss ten fair coins (ten coins in the air at the same time) an infinite number of times we will get an orderly distribution of this random event. This distribution can be graphed, and the numbers in the graph can be tabled. The probability of either a head or a tail on any <u>single</u> coin toss is .5.

Figure 5 demonstrates the theoretical probability distribution of the ten coin toss event, based on an infinite number of tosses. The theoretical probability of 5 heads and 5 tails is .246; the probability of either 4 heads/6 tails or 6 heads/4 tails is .205; and the probability of 7/3 or 3/7 is .117; the probability of 8/2 or 2/8 is .044; the probability of 9/1 or 1/9 is .010; and finally the probability of 10/0 or 0/10 is .001. Where do these probability fractions come from? Computer programs can be set up to simulate the tossing of ten fair coins an "infinite" (a large enough number of times to simulate infinity) number of times. When the ten coins are tossed an infinite number of times almost 25% (.246) of the ten coin outcomes will be 5 heads and 5 tails. These events (5 heads and 5 tails, 6 heads and 4 tails, and so on) and their associated theoretical probabilities together make up the binomial distribution.

A STATISTICAL TABLE BUILT UPON RANDOM COIN TOSSES

EVENT	0H 10T	1H 9T	2H 8T	3H 7T	4H 6T	5H 5T	6H 4T	7H 3T	8H 2T	9H 1T	10H 0T
PROBABILITY OF EVENT OCCURING	.001	.010	.044	.117	.205	.246	.205	.117	.044	.010	.001

H = HEADS
T = TAILS

FIGURE 5

If you wanted to judge the fairness of a coin, you could toss the coin ten times, and then compare your results with the binomial distribution in Figure 5. If you got 5 heads and 5 tails, or either a 6/4 or 4/6 split, or even a 7/3 or 3/7 split, you could reasonably assume the coin was fair. However, if you got an 8/2 or 2/8, 9/1 or 1/9, or 10/0 or 0/10 split, then the coin is unlikely to be fair. Why? Because the theoretical probability of achieving any of these splits with a fair coin is less than .05. If you got any of these extreme splits it is likely that the coin is not "fair"- something other than randomness determined the results.

The results of any sample study are analogous to tossing a set of ten coins a single time. The results are compared to a table of randomly determined probabilities that are derived from a theoretical distribution based on the universe of all possible outcomes of the event being studied.

As stated above, the binomial distribution is a nonparametric, non-normal distribution based on a qualitative, discrete, categorical event. In addition to the binomial distribution there are many other theoretical non-normal population distributions. The binomial distribution is usually chosen as the one non-normal distribution to present in detail in introductory statistics because it mimics certain characteristics of parametric, normal distributions.

How can a discrete, either/or event, such as a coin toss, be related to the normal distribution, which is based on continuous data? As we just demonstrated, even though any given coin toss is a discrete event, the curve that maps this binomial event is based on the outcome distribution of many coin tosses.

When one tosses ten coins, each of the possible proportions of heads and tails has a certain <u>probability</u> of occurrence by chance, as stated above. The right hand graph shown in Figure 6 demonstrates that these probabilities can be approximated by a <u>bell shaped curve</u>. The bell shaped curve is one of the defining characteristics of normal distributions. Figure 6 demonstrates that the bell shaped curve is only an approximation of the distribution of the coin toss example. Why is this so? The events are discrete; the event is either 0 heads/10 tails, or 1 head/9 tails, and so on. As such, the graph is simply composed of vertical bars increasing in height toward the center of the distribution. The curve is smooth and continuous, and the data from the coin toss example only touch or approach the curve at certain points. If we had mapped out a 100 coin toss event, there would be many more bars, and many more of them would touch or approach the curve. The right hand side of Figure 6 shows how even a 20 coin toss event would have many more bars touching or approaching the curve. <u>However, no matter how many discrete events one maps, the distribution would still be bars that would only approximate the normal curve.</u> It is only with continuous, parametric data, with its infinite divisibility, that probable occurrences of events can be thought of as actually touching every point on a bell shaped curve.

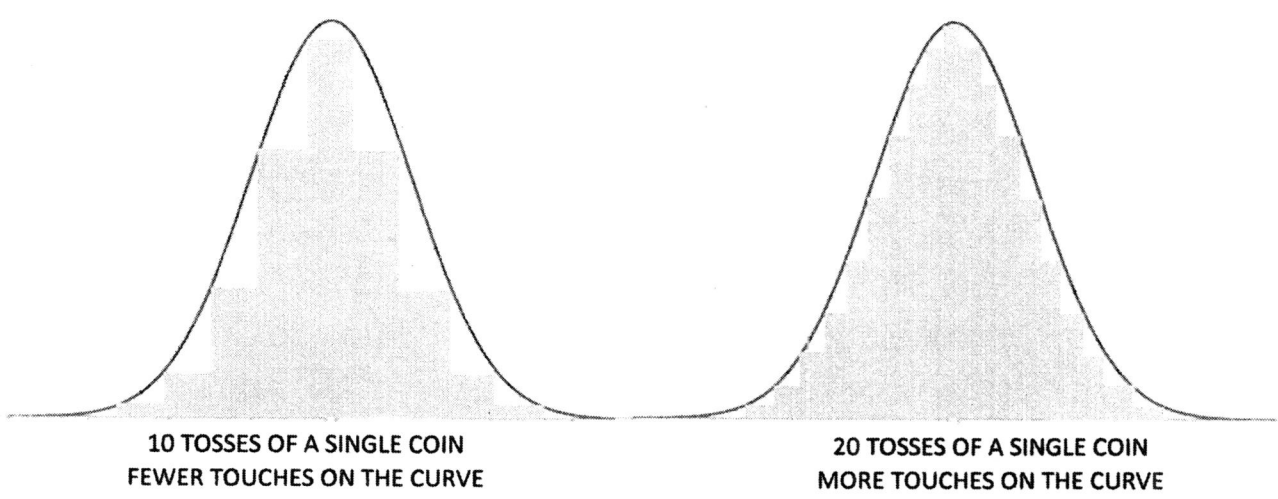

10 TOSSES OF A SINGLE COIN
FEWER TOUCHES ON THE CURVE

20 TOSSES OF A SINGLE COIN
MORE TOUCHES ON THE CURVE

FIGURE 6

E. The bell shaped normal curve of a parametric distribution

Continuous events or characteristics often fall into approximately normal distributions at the population level. Normally distributed random variables are parametric, continuous, quantitative, arbitrarily categorical, and symmetrical about their centers. The characteristic symmetrical bell shape of the normal distribution means that most values on the continuum are in the center of the distribution, with an equally declining number of values going away form the center on either side of the center. Unlike the binomial event approximation of the bell shaped curve, all the values in a normal distribution actually touch the curve at all points along the curve.

The curve that maps the theoretical normal distribution is shown in Figure 7. The normal distribution is drawn in a two dimensional graph, with the frequencies or percentages on the Y axis and scores of the variable on the X axis. If the values of the variable are perfectly normally distributed, then 50% of the values will fall on either side of the center of the distribution.

Why is the bell shaped curve shown in Figure 7 called "normal"? It is called normal because many characteristics relevant to humans are continuous, and can be accurately mapped by the curve. These characteristics range from physical features, such as height, weight, and shoe size, to aptitude measures, such as intelligence, and to personality characteristics such as shyness and neuroticism. Measuring any of these characteristics at the population (huge sample) level would lead approximately to the distribution shown in Figure 7.

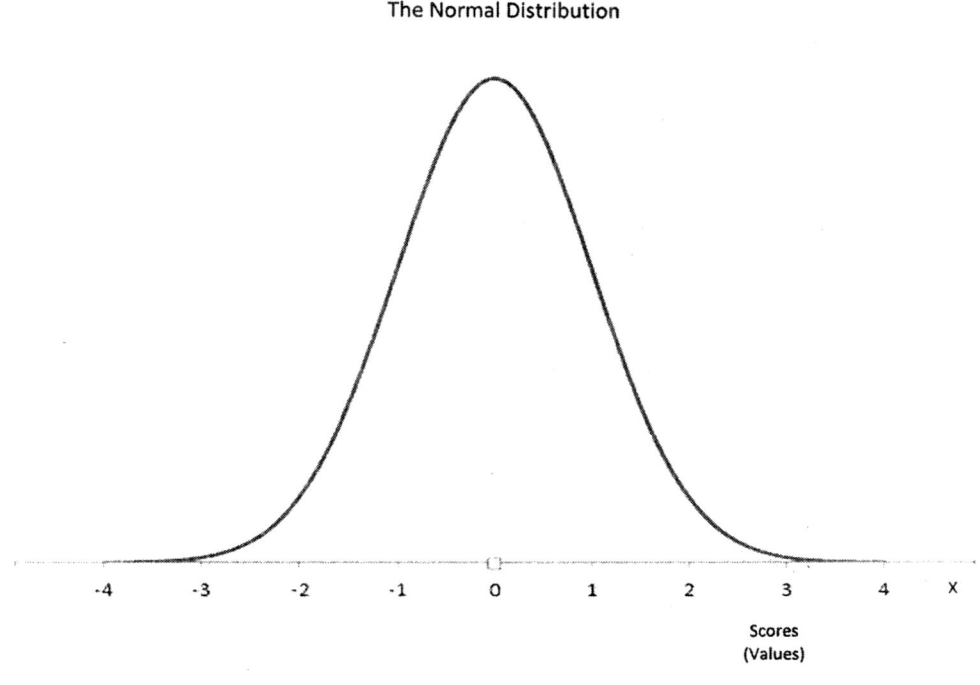

FIGURE 7

Chapter Summary

Sample data are collected on either a parametric or nonparametric variable, and numbers representing the data are placed in an inference test formula. The number generated from manipulating the formula is compared to a number in the statistical table for that inference test. We now know that the table represents the random population distribution of values for the variable on which sample data were gathered. The comparison leads to the probability statement, and the probability statement tells us whether the results of the study are significant or not. This is why statistical tables, and the random assumed population distributions that the tables are built upon, are so important. Without the random population distributions there is nothing to compare the sample data distribution against, and therefore the sample to population inference process could not occur, and a probability statement could not be generated. Researchers would not bother with the sample to population inference process unless they thought there was a possibility of identifying a causal relation at the population level. The next chapter discusses how ideas about causality at the population level are integrated into the sample to population inference process.

Concept 4 states that sample data are assumed to come from populations with characteristic distributions that are either parametric or nonparametric. Parametric distributions are bell shaped (normal), and the values in the distribution come from event, object or organism characteristics that are continuous, not discrete. Nonparametric distributions are not normal, and the values in the distribution come from discrete characteristics.

Chapter 5:

Order vs. Disorder: The Alternative versus Null Hypothesis

<u>**Chapter Outline**</u>

Chapter Preview
Review
Concept 5

<u>**Chapter Summary**</u>

Chapter Preview

Review

Concept 1 states that, unless empirically proven otherwise, the causes of events are assumed to be complex, unknown, and random. The null hypothesis is based on this assumption set. The researcher's hypothesis regarding the event of interest is never proposed in a vacuum, but always as an alternative to the null hypothesis. Given the uncertainties in the sample to population inference process (Concepts 2 and 3), the rules for accepting an alternative hypothesis and rejecting the null hypothesis are very stringent, and the acceptance of the alternative is never absolute.

The numbers that result from manipulating the inference test formulas are compared to the appropriate statistical table numbers to see if the probability statement is statistically significant, which would indicate that the assumption that the sample data come from a random population distribution is incorrect (Concept 4). We shall see in this chapter that this comparison is captured in the context of the alternative versus the null hypothesis.

Concept 5: If there is more than one possible cause to any event at the population level, then it is possible to divide these causes into the presumably nonrandom cause of interest (the alternative hypothesis) and all other, presumably random, causes (the null hypothesis).

Dividing the causes of events into the presumably nonrandom cause of interest (the alternative hypothesis) and all other, presumably random, causes (the null hypothesis) allows for the usage of sample data to infer to the population level in order to determine probabilistically which of the hypotheses is correct.

In this chapter you will learn that the null and alternative hypotheses are operationally and numerically defined in statistical inference test formulas: <u>all statistical inference formulas contain numerical representatives of the null and alternative hypotheses</u>. Later in the chapter you will learn that the parametric and nonparametric population random variable distributions discussed in the last chapter help to specifically structure the null and alternative hypotheses for each research study.

A. The null versus the alternative hypothesis.

The word <u>null</u> means "of no consequence, effect, or value; insignificant"; or, "amounting to nothing; lacking, absent, nonexistent." The null hypothesis states that whatever causal relation a researcher discovers at the sample level does not exist at the population level, because at that level no variable will have a consistent, causal effect on any other variable. The null hypothesis assumes that the sample results are simply due to error; that is, to unknown, presumably random factors. Therefore any causal relations discovered at the sample level must be a mistake, which repeated sampling would reveal.

The null hypothesis is based on the Concept 1 assumption discussed in Chapter 1, that the universe is random and that there are no causal relations at the universal or population level, unless empirically proven otherwise. The null hypothesis means that, in research, there are no intuitively accepted causal relations. In research causal relations must be empirically proven <u>against</u> the null hypothesis and the assumption that the universe is random.

Given the underlying assumption of randomness that defines the null hypothesis, research is always the process of testing an alternative hypothesis against the null hypothesis. Alternative means alternative to the null hypothesis. A hypothesis is defined as "a conjecture that accounts, within a theoretical framework, for a set of facts and that can be used as a basis of further investigation". The alternative hypothesis is the researcher's educated guess about what will happen in a study. More specifically, the researcher hypothesizes a nonrandom, causal relation at the population level. Calling this hypothesis the alternative hypothesis means that researchers never hypothesize in a vacuum. To put it in perceptual terms, the alternative hypothesis is the narrow beam of illumination from a flashlight, and the null hypothesis is the all-encompassing darkness surrounding the beam.

Perhaps you would like to test the alternative hypothesis that drinking coffee before an exam increases test performance. In your study the null hypothesis is that coffee drinking has no causal relation to test performance at the population level. In your study you randomly sample from the students on campus and randomly assign them to either a coffee drinking or a no coffee drinking condition. You then give both groups a test, and you analyze the data to see which group has the better exam performance. The null hypothesis would be supported if there turns out to be no difference in the performance of the two groups. The alternative would be supported if the coffee drinking group has better performance. However, since the research process and hypothesis testing are based on sample observation and inductive logic, neither the null or alternative hypothesis can ever be proven to be absolutely true or false. There are probabilities assigned to both of the outcomes attached to these mutually exclusive hypotheses, and these two probabilities always add up to 1.

B. The null hypothesis, probability, and inference errors.

Examine the three charts in Figure 8. These charts demonstrate how the null and the alternative hypotheses are related to probability, and to the sampling process. The various charts compare the universal (population) and sample levels. At the universal level, which is empirically unknowable by humans, the null hypothesis could be <u>either</u> true or false. We are only assuming that it is true. Non-significant results do not always mean that the null hypothesis is true. Similarly, significant results do not always mean that the null hypothesis is false, because there is <u>always</u> at least a small possibility that randomness determined your significant sample results.

	UNIVERSAL (POPULATION) LEVEL (UNKNOWN TO HUMANS)	SAMPLE LEVEL (KNOWN TO HUMANS)	ERROR?
THEORETICAL	NULL TRUE	NONSIGNIFICANT RESULTS	NO
	NULL TRUE	SIGNIFICANT RESULTS	TYPE I ERROR (POSITIVE)
	NULL FALSE	SIGNIFICANT RESULTS	NO
	NULL FALSE	NONSIGNIFICANT RESULTS	TYPE II ERROR (NEGATIVE)
DRUG EXAMPLE	DRUG INEFFECTIVE (NULL TRUE)	NONSIGNIFICANT RESULTS	NO
	DRUG INEFFECTIVE (NULL TRUE)	SIGNIFICANT RESULTS	TYPE I ERROR (RELEASE INEFFECTIVE DRUG)
	DRUG BENEFICIAL (NULL FALSE)	SIGNIFICANT RESULTS	NO
	DRUG BENEFICIAL (NULL FALSE)	NONSIGNIFICANT RESULTS	TYPE II ERROR (DENY BENEFICIAL DRUG)
HUNTER EXAMPLE	RANDOM NOISE (NULL TRUE)	EARPLUGS	NO
	RANDOM NOISE (NULL TRUE)	NO EARPLUGS	TYPE I ERROR (HEARS RANDOM NOISES)
	TIGER NOISE (NULL FALSE	NO EARPLUGS	NO
	TIGER NOISE (NULL FALSE	EARPLUGS	TYPE II ERROR (TIGER EATS HUNTER)

FIGURE 8

However, we do know what happened at the sample level where the data are actually collected. At the sample level results can either be significant or non-significant, leading to the possibility of two types of errors in the inference process. In a <u>Type I error</u> researchers "read too much into the data," assuming that their significant results mean the null hypothesis is false. In a Type II error researchers have "not read enough into the data," mistaking non-significant results for a true null hypothesis at the population level. Because of probability, researchers can never reduce the possibility of these errors to zero. The only choice researchers have is to increase or decrease the possibility of one type of error versus the other type. Changing the ratio of Type I and Type II errors is done by changing the probability level boundary between significant and non-significant results.

The drug and hunter example charts in Figure 8 demonstrate the implications of setting the probability level (known as the alpha level) that separates statistically significant from non-significant results at particular locations between 0 and 1. If the alpha level is set at .05 or .20, which type of error will be diminished and which one will be encouraged?

The probability of a Type I error is set by alpha, the significance level. In other words, if the results of a study lead to a probability of .05, there are still 5 chances out of 100 that the results occurred by chance, and that the null hypothesis is true. An alpha level of .01 or .05 indicates that the scientific community is biased against Type I errors, and would rather make Type II errors than Type I errors. Why is this so? An alpha of .01 or .05 means that it is difficult to achieve significant results. Therefore the results of most, or at least more, studies are non-significant, thereby increasing the chances of a Type II error and decreasing the chances of Type I. If alpha were set at .20 it would be easier to achieve significant results and there would be fewer studies with non-significant results, thereby changing the Type I/Type II error proportions.

Why are researchers so restrictive regarding significant results? The answer to this question is important since statistical significance is the gateway to acceptance of results as empirical knowledge or fact. Perhaps the drug example charted in Figure 8 can help answer this question. In drug studies the alpha is often set at .01 rather than .05, which makes it even harder to get significant results. Society and the scientific community have made a decision regarding drugs: It is considered far worse to unleash a potentially dangerous drug on society (Type I error) than to deprive society of a potentially beneficial drug (Type II error). In general we are much more willing to risk losing important knowledge than to accept results that are not "true" at the population level. The .05 or .01 arbitrary boundary between significant and non-significant results favors the conservative experimenter, who is more willing to risk "not seeing enough in the data," than to risk "seeing too much in the data."

Are there examples where a Type II error would be considered more harmful? In the third example charted in Figure 8, a hunter is out in the forest. He is spending his first night alone and he is having difficulty sleeping because he keeps hearing noises. These noises could be random forest noise (null hypothesis) or could be tigers moving about (alternative hypothesis). He solves the problem by putting earplugs in his ears to shut out the noises, only to be attacked and eaten by a tiger!

What has he done, in statistical terminology? He has reduced the possibility of a Type I error, making it less likely that he will hear random noises. The earplugs, while reducing the possibility of Type I error, increases the possibility of a Type II error, making it more likely that he will not hear tiger noises.

To summarize, when researchers collect data from a sample there is the possibility of either a Type I or Type II error, depending on whether the results are statistically significant or not. The fact that we strive not to make Type I errors, even at the expense of having more Type II errors, demonstrates the deep influence of the null hypothesis in research. <u>The null hypothesis is the basic hypothesis</u>. It not only influences how research studies are planned and executed; it also influences the numerical tables that determine whether the results of those studies are significant or not.

C. Statistical Power

The charts in Figure 8 demonstrate a concept related to the null and alternative hypotheses; statistical power. <u>Statistical power</u> is defined as the probability of rejecting a null hypothesis that is in fact false. Statistical power is associated with a particular cell in each of the charts in Figure 8. In that cell the sample results are significant and at the universal level the null hypothesis is false, leading to the correct decision to reject the null hypothesis. Increased statistical power is desired by every researcher. In terms of a simple formula, statistical power can be defined as 1 minus the probability of a Type II error.

Therefore if researchers want to increase power it would appear that they simply need to decrease the probability of Type II errors. However, if researchers decrease the probability of Type II errors they will increase the probability of Type I errors! Therefore researchers look for ways to increase statistical power other than by adjusting the alpha level. Power can be increased by changing certain factors in the research design, such as by increasing the sample size, and by assuming that the underlying population distribution is parametric rather than nonparametric.

D. How the null and alternative hypotheses are related to the assumed population distribution

We learned in Chapter 4 that every inference test, whether based on parametric or nonparametric data, has a corresponding statistical table. Each table is composed of numbers associated with probability values. These values indicate how likely it is that a particular number would be generated on a random basis, for the particular event being tested. The probabilities associated with the various random values of the event have a characteristic distribution.

The null hypothesis is structured to fit the distributions incorporated into the various statistical tables. The null hypothesis states that the results of a study are randomly generated, that the results will lead to a formula number that matches a table number likely to have been generated randomly, and therefore the matched numbers will be associated with a probability value greater than .05 (or .01, if the alpha level is set at .01). The alternative hypothesis states that study results will lead to a formula number that matches a table number that was very unlikely to have been generated randomly, thus leading to a probability statement of less than .05.

For events measured parametrically, the normal distribution, or a distribution closely related to the normal distribution, defines the range of values that lead to either the retention or rejection of the null hypothesis (and therefore the rejection or acceptance of the alternative hypothesis). Figure 9 demonstrates graphically how the normal distribution is used to retain or reject the null hypothesis when the alpha level is set at .05. The vast majority of the area under the curve is labeled as the "area of retention of the null hypothesis (rejection of the alternative hypothesis)." The two very small areas, one located toward each of the distribution tails, are labeled the "areas of rejection of the null hypothesis (acceptance of the alternative hypothesis)." The demarcation between the areas of retention and rejection is set by the chosen alpha level, in this case .05. The numbers and the associated probability values in the Z table are based on this distribution.

For the nonparametric binomial event, the non-normal binomial distribution defines the null and alternative hypotheses, and for other nonparametric events other non-normal distributions, such as the chi square distribution, define the null and alternative hypotheses.

E. Most statistical inference tests contain numbers representing the null and the alternative hypotheses.

We now know that the multiple explanations for any event can be placed into two categories. Sample data represent an event that resulted from either a random accident (including all other possible causes other than the one of interest to the researcher) represented by the null hypothesis, or the specific non-random cause of interest to the researcher, represented by the alternative hypothesis. Perhaps it might be useful to think of the null versus alternative hypothesis as a struggle between these two categories, between randomness and order. Inference test formulas play out this struggle numerically. Most tests contain numerical components that represent both the alternative and the null hypothesis, and these components are pitted against each other. The purpose of any formula calculation is to see which components are larger.

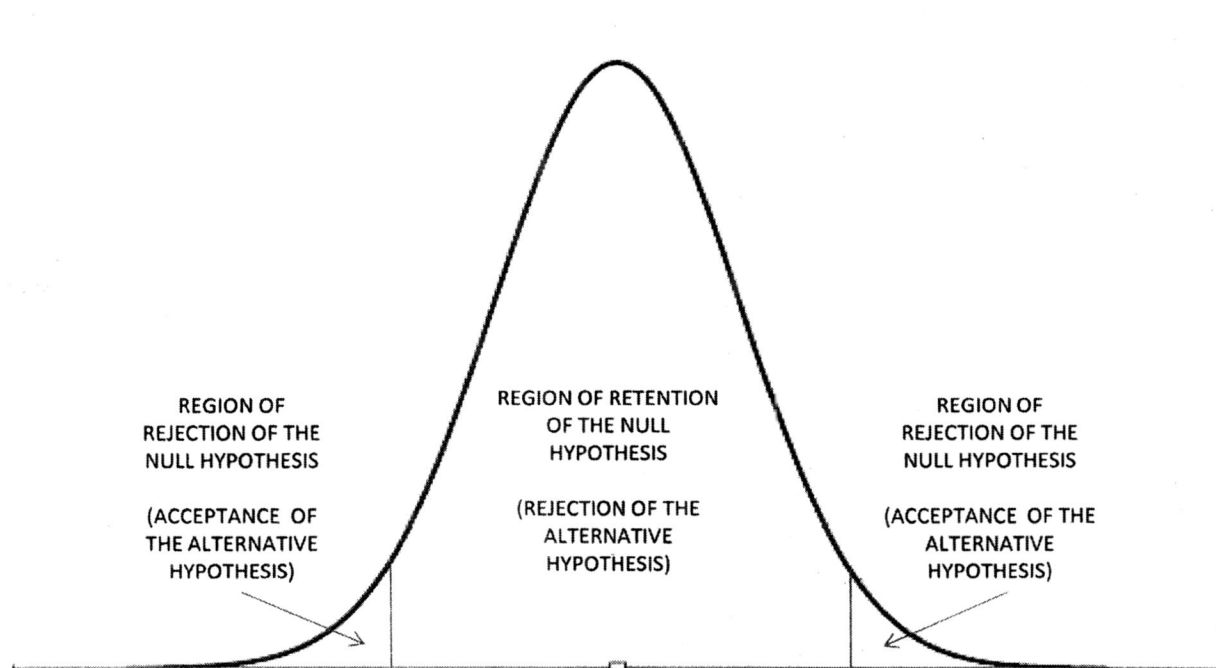

THE NORMAL DISTRIBUTION

REGION OF REJECTION OF THE NULL HYPOTHESIS

(ACCEPTANCE OF THE ALTERNATIVE HYPOTHESIS)

REGION OF RETENTION OF THE NULL HYPOTHESIS

(REJECTION OF THE ALTERNATIVE HYPOTHESIS)

REGION OF REJECTION OF THE NULL HYPOTHESIS

(ACCEPTANCE OF THE ALTERNATIVE HYPOTHESIS)

NOTE: THIS FIGURE ASSUMES A TWO TAILED (NONDIRECTIONAL) ALTERNATIVE HYPOTHESIS THAT DIVIDES THE REGION OF REJECTION BETWEEN THE TWO TAILS OF THE DISTRIBUTION.

FIGURE 9

The Z test is usually the first inference test formula learned by students in an introductory statistics course. The numerator of the Z test is shown in Figure 10. X bar, the sample mean, is a descriptive statistic derived from sample data, and μ, the population mean, is derived from population data. The population mean represents the null hypothesis because, according to the null hypothesis, all variables operating at the population level are random. The sample mean represents the alternative hypothesis because it numerically represents the experimental treatment or intervention. The sample mean is our best numerical guess for demonstrating that an intervention or treatment would work at a population level. The bigger the sample mean the more distinct it will be from the assumed population mean and the more likely it is that the researcher will be able to reject the null and accept the alternative hypothesis.

As a hypothetical example, you have formulated a new "smart" drug that you believe will substantially raise IQ scores. You persuade a group of 15 friends to take the new supplement. You then give each of them an IQ test and formulate the sample mean, which turns out to be 107. Given that the "population" mean IQ is 100 (a number based on the IQ testing of a huge sample of millions of people) you figure you might have something here. However, 107 is not that different from 100. The sample results could have easily been achieved simply by sampling error, by random chance factors involved in picking that particular sample. It is unlikely that the administration of your drug at the population level would change the population mean IQ. However, what if your sample mean turned out to be 140? Now the difference between the sample mean and the population mean is 40, not 7. It is more likely that you can reject the null hypothesis and accept the alternative, knowing that your risk of being wrong is very small. If you administered the drug to the population it is likely that the population IQ mean would shift substantially upward.

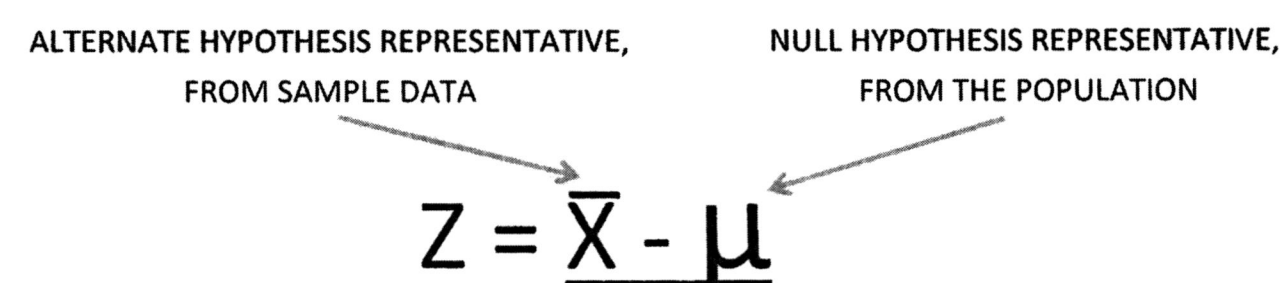

ALTERNATE HYPOTHESIS REPRESENTATIVE, FROM SAMPLE DATA

NULL HYPOTHESIS REPRESENTATIVE, FROM THE POPULATION

$$Z = \underline{\bar{X} - \mu}$$

FIGURE 10

Some of you already know that this example has not made use of the complete Z test formula. The example only used the numerator portion of the test;

there is a denominator portion as well. The denominator contains the population standard deviation. The standard deviation is a measure of the dispersion of scores away from the center of a distribution in either a sample or population distribution.

Chapter Summary

The process of hypothesis testing is usually framed as testing the researcher's hypothesis about a possible causal relation at the population level. This is misleading because it implies that the researcher's hypothesis is the only hypothesis in consideration in a research study. In fact, in every study the researcher's hypothesis is always the second hypothesis under consideration. The hypothesis that is typically not stated, the null hypothesis, is based on randomness and is always the first hypothesis to be considered. The null hypothesis should be more openly discussed in introductory statistics books because every inference test formula contains numbers that represent both the null and alternative (researcher's) hypotheses. These representative numbers are typically pitted against each other to see which hypothesis is probabilistically likely to be more representative of the population level.

Chapter 6 will further your understanding of the alterative versus the null hypothesis by introducing two concepts from the field of communication: signal and noise. When you communicate with someone you want your message to be interpreted accurately by the receiver of the message. This can be accomplished by increasing the strength of the signal (the actual content of the message) and by decreasing the noise (the static or other distracting events that are occurring at the same time as your message). The numerator of the Z test is a signal, and the denominator, the measure of dispersion, is noise.

Chapter 6:

Signal Versus Noise and Inference Tests

Chapter Outline

Chapter Preview
Review
Concept 6

    A. Signal vs. Noise: how most formulas are constructed
    B. Acceptance of the Alternative vs. the Null Hypothesis

Chapter Summary

Chapter Preview

Review

Concept 1 states that all events at the universal (population) level have more than one possible cause and effect, that most of these causes and effects are unknown, and that the causes and effects are random, unless empirically proven otherwise. Concept 2 states that population events are never observed by humans; our observations occur at the sample level. Therefore to empirically prove causal relations at the universal level, researchers must infer from a sample of event observations to the total population of potential event observations.

Furthermore, if all events have random and multiple effects (outcomes) at the population level, then Concept 3 states that the outcome of any single unobserved event can only be conceived in terms of probabilities, not absolutes.

Concept 4 states that sample data, and the descriptive statistics derived from the sample data, are assumed to come from random variables (event or entity) populations where the characteristic patterns are assumed to have either parametric or nonparametric distributions. Concept 5 states that if there is more than one possible cause to any event at the population level, then it is possible to divide these causes into the presumed nonrandom cause of interest (the alternative hypothesis) and all other, presumably random, causes (the null hypothesis).

Concept 6

If a number indicating the outcome of the comparison of the null vs. the alternative hypothesis is the signal in inference tests, then a measure of dispersion is noise.

This chapter will introduce a concept from communication research, signal vs. noise, and apply it to inference formulas. The outcome of the struggle between the alternative and null hypotheses discussed in Chapter 5 constitutes the signal, and the variability inherent in all sample measurement constitutes noise.

In statistics noise is called either random error or variability. Thinking of variability as noise implies that variability obscures a signal. What would be a signal in statistics? Any descriptive statistic summarizing the values that cluster at the center of a distribution, such as a mean, could be a signal.

A. Signal vs. Noise: how most formulas are constructed

The signal vs. noise concept from communications can be helpful in understanding inference tests. Figure 11 shows four possible relations between signal and noise. In communication the signal is the meaningful message or transmission. Signals are pictured here as symmetrical curvilinear lines with large swings between peaks and valleys, which vary in strength, as demonstrated by the thickness and darkness of the lines. Noise, the meaningless, random transmission, is drawn as lines with reduced peaks and valleys. Noise also varies in strength, as shown by the variation in thickness and darkness of the lines. Figure 11 demonstrates four possible combinations of signal and noise: strong signal/strong noise, weak signal/strong noise, strong signal/weak noise, and weak signal/weak noise. These four possibilities vary in desirability. A communicator would ideally like a strong signal with weak noise, the upper right cell in Figure 11. The communicator's nightmare is the lower left cell, with a weak signal and strong noise; the other two cells are intermediate in desirability.

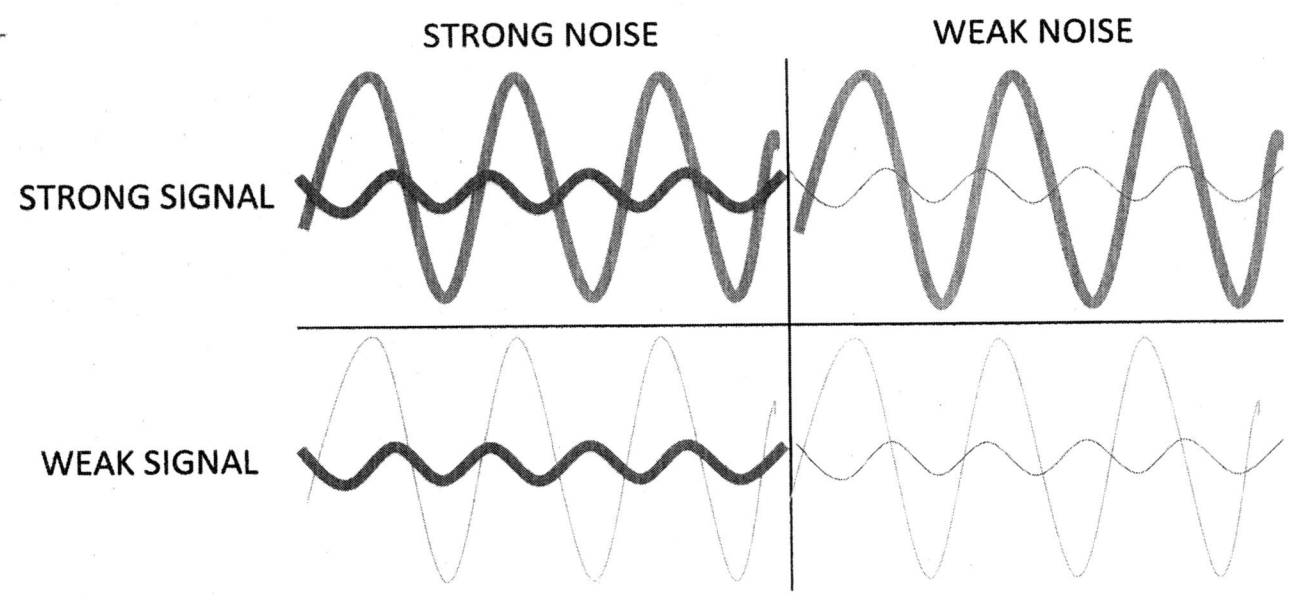

FIGURE 11

What does this signal-noise analogy have to do with research and statistics? You are attending a lecture in a classroom with only one exit. While everyone is listening attentively to the lecturer, suddenly flames and smoke burst from the ceiling in the back of the room. What is everyone's first inclination? Of course, to run to the one door! This example shows that sometimes a cause is so strong that it has a powerful and uniform effect on everyone. The flames and smoke are powerful and intense enough to cause everyone to immediately run to the door.

Let's compare this with a different variation of the same situation. Now there are just a few little wisps of smoke emerging from the ceiling in the back of the room. How would people in the classroom react to this? Some would turn and look at the smoke, some would ignore it, some would laugh about it, some would talk about it, someone might ask the lecturer about it, and so on. This cause is not strong enough to evoke a uniform response from everyone. Wisps of smoke, unlike strong flames and smoke, will not suppress individual differences. There will be a wide variety of responses to the wisps, whereas there will be little variety of response to the strong flames and smoke. The strong flames and smoke equates to a strong signal, and the wisps of smoke equate to a weak signal. Every researcher's dream is to have a strong signal, a causal variable that influences everyone to act in the same way.

Similarly, every researcher wishes to control research conditions enough so that noise is suppressed. What is noise in our example? First, some people in the classroom will be more alert, others less so. Some will be more or less anxious, more or less sensitive, and so on. Second, the building heating system could have run amok, so that certain portions of the classroom became extremely cold and other portions extremely hot, before the smoke appeared in the ceiling. Third, if the classroom had numerous doors, and windows opening onto a ground floor it is not likely that everyone would run to just one door, no matter how strong the flames and smoke.

These examples indicate that in research noise reflects (1) all the individual differences in various characteristics that people bring to any situation; (2) the presence of random variability in environmental variables present in the experimental situation, and (3) the presence of other, uncontrolled variables that are unknown competing signals which weaken the strength of the cause-effect relation under consideration. If these noise factors are present there will be increasing variation in the way individuals respond to any given causal variable. The process of exerting control in research is an attempt to strengthen signal and suppress noise.

Since only one number is usually used to represent the alternative hypothesis portion of the signal, the validity of that number becomes crucially important. Validity is defined as actually measuring what you say you are measuring.

Asking if the sample data, and the numerical summaries of that data that represent the alternative hypothesis, are representative of a population level event is the same as asking if the sample data are valid.

The basic form of most inference test formulas, shown in Figure 12, constructs a signal by subtracting the null hypothesis representative from the alternative hypothesis representative, and then divides the signal by the noise representative. This basic formula model provides two opportunities to test the validity of the alternative hypothesis representative.

BASIC STRUCTURE OF MOST INFERENCE TEST FORMULAS:

$$\frac{\text{SIGNAL (ALTERNATIVE - NULL)}}{\text{NOISE}}$$

FIGURE 12

Two validity test opportunities are provided because the null hypothesis has two numerical representatives in the formula. One numerical representative of the null hypothesis (such as the population mean in the Z test) has already been discussed in the last chapter, and it is subtracted from the alternative hypothesis representative. Applying the concept of noise to research means that the null hypothesis is represented in this basic inference test formula model a second time. Noise is assumed to be random, and randomness is the key element in the concept of the null hypothesis.

In the formula model the number representing noise is divided into the signal because in research, as in communication, noise detracts from the clarity of the signal. No matter how hard we attempt to exert control, the attempt never totally succeeds. Causal variables (signals) will never be perfectly strong, and variability (noise) caused by random and uncontrolled variables and individual differences will never be totally suppressed. All inference tests are measures of our success (or lack of) in creating research situations of strong signals and weak noise. The purpose of inference tests is to measure the relative strength of signal and noise in a given research project.

Now we can return to the example first introduced in Chapter 5. Your friends took your new "smart" drug, took an IQ test and the sample average was 107. Since this IQ is somewhat above 100, you use the Z formula to test your alternative hypothesis that this new drug would substantially improve intelligence at the population level.

The full, numerator and denominator, Z test formula is given in Figure 13. The signal is derived by subtracting the null hypothesis representative, the population mean, from the alternative hypothesis representative, the sample mean. In our example 100 is subtracted from 107, then the remainder of 7 is divided by 15. Where does the 15 come from and what does it represent?

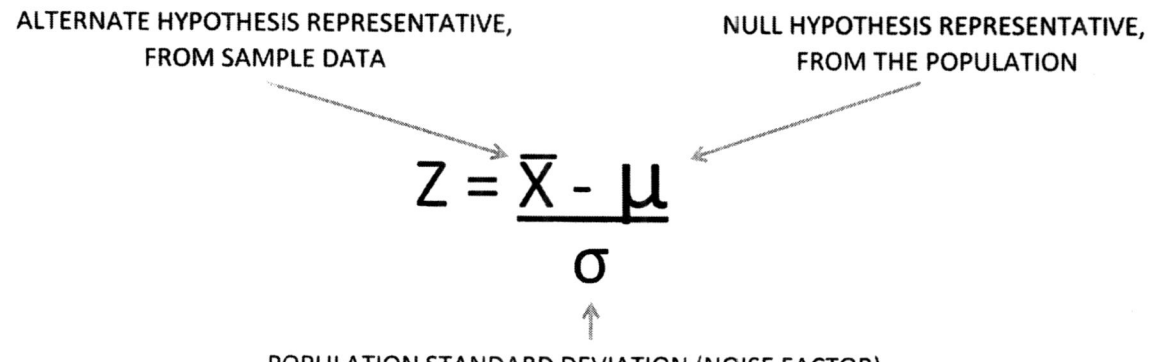

ALTERNATE HYPOTHESIS REPRESENTATIVE, FROM SAMPLE DATA

NULL HYPOTHESIS REPRESENTATIVE, FROM THE POPULATION

$$Z = \frac{\bar{X} - \mu}{\sigma}$$

POPULATION STANDARD DEVIATION (NOISE FACTOR)

FIGURE 13

Fifteen is the population standard deviation. This IQ "population" standard deviation, like the IQ "population" mean, is derived from sampling millions of individuals. It is extremely unlikely that we will ever come up with a causal event so strong that everyone will react the same way to that event. Most causal events used in research have more in common with "wisps of smoke" than with "smoke and flames"! Since people will have different reactions to any causal event, there needs to be numerical measures of the variety of their reactions. The standard deviation is such a measure. Since the variability in response to a causal event is noise, the standard deviation is a numerical measure of noise. In communication and in statistics noise obscures the clarity of the signal. Therefore the noise representative, the standard deviation, is the denominator in the Z test formula. The denominator, noise, is divided into the numerator, signal. The effect of noise is to reduce the size (clarity) of the signal.

In our example we divide 7 by 15, giving a Z of .47. Or, if your sample mean was 140, you would subtract 100 from 140, and divide 40 by 15, giving you a Z score of 2.67. What do either of these Z scores mean in terms of probability and accepting or rejecting either the null or alternative hypotheses?

B. Acceptance of the Null vs. the Alternative

Once a formula number is derived by dividing Signal by Noise, acceptance of either the alternative or null hypothesis is based on a comparison of the formula number to the appropriate table number. A number which is the result of mathematically manipulating an inference test formula is compared to an appropriate table number for that particular test, in order to derive a probability statement and therefore conclude whether the alternative hypothesis is accepted or the null hypothesis is retained. For example, a Z test result is compared to a number in the Z table, a t test result to a number in the t table, a chi square test result to a number in the chi square table, and so on. The formula number usually needs to be equal to or bigger than the table number in order to reject the null hypothesis and accept the alternative hypothesis.

Figuratively (Figure 14) speaking, the formula number must "hurdle" over the table number to achieve statistical significance at the chosen alpha level probability. The probability statement tells us, in numerical terms, the possibility that the event was determined by chance/random factors. To accept an alternative hypothesis, the probability assigned to chance must be low.

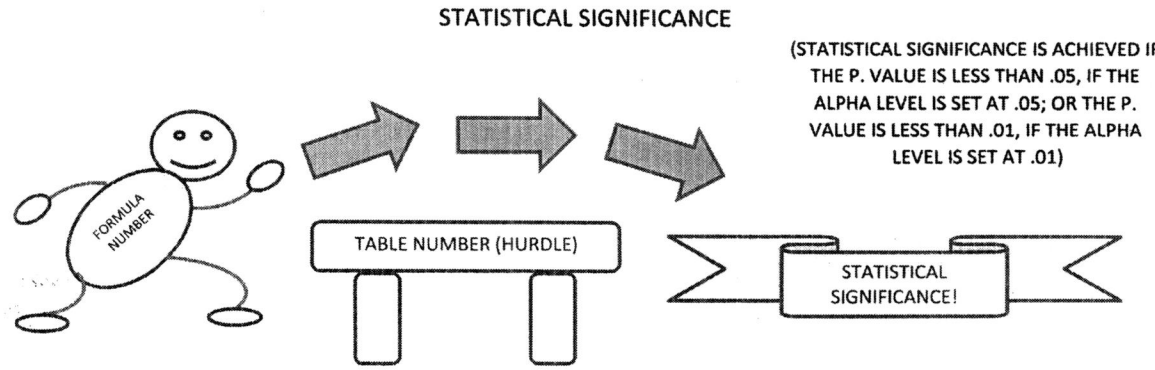

STATISTICAL SIGNIFICANCE

(STATISTICAL SIGNIFICANCE IS ACHIEVED IF THE P. VALUE IS LESS THAN .05, IF THE ALPHA LEVEL IS SET AT .05; OR THE P. VALUE IS LESS THAN .01, IF THE ALPHA LEVEL IS SET AT .01)

TABLE NUMBER (HURDLE)

STATISTICAL SIGNIFICANCE!

IF THE FORMULA NUMBER IS BIGGER THAN (HURDLES OVER) THE COMPARISON TABLE NUMBER, THEN STATISTICAL SIGNIFICANCE IS ACHIEVED, AND THE NULL HYPOTHESIS CAN BE REJECTED AND THE ALTERNATIVE HYPOTHESIS ACCEPTED

FIGURE 14

Now you can finally find out whether your "smart" drug is worthy of major investment. If your sample mean IQ was 107 your Z score was .47. You now compare your formula derived number, .47, to the appropriate table number in the Z table in the back of a standard statistics textbook. At the .05 alpha level the appropriate table number is 1.65. Your formula derived number, .47, is definitely not "hurdling" over this table number! You cannot reject the null hypothesis and accept the alternative. It is likely that your sample results were due to random variation. What if your sample mean IQ had been 140, with a Z score of 2.67? 2.67 definitely does hurdle over the appropriate table number, 1.65. Here you have statistically significant results with a probability of less than .05. You can safely reject the null hypothesis and accept the alternative hypothesis, knowing that it is unlikely that these results were achieved by chance. It is likely that if the population used your smart drug the population IQ would rise.

Chapter Summary

The signal and noise concepts allow us to fully understand the basic structure of inference test formulas. The signal in a formula is created by comparing the numerical representatives of the alternative versus the null hypotheses, and then the signal is divided by the measure of noise, representing dispersion or variability.

In this chapter the Z inference test formula was used in the example. However, as you probably know by now, there are many different statistical inference test formulas. How do you decide which one to use to test your alternative hypothesis against the null hypothesis? The answer to this question is the topic of Chapter 7.

Chapter 7:

Layered Inference: Levels of Measurement

Chapter Preview

Review

Concept 1 states that all events at the universal (population) level have more than one possible cause and effect, that most of these causes and effects are unknown, and that the causes and effects are random, unless empirically proven otherwise. Concept 2 states that events are never observed at the universal (population) level, always at the sample level. Therefore, to empirically prove causal relations at the universal level, researchers must infer from a sample of event observations to the total population of potential event observations. If all events have random and multiple effects (outcomes) at the population level, then Concept 3 states that the outcome of any single unobserved event can only be conceived in terms of probabilities, not absolutes.

Concept 4 indicates that sample data, and the descriptive statistics derived from sample data, are assumed to come from random variable (event or entity) populations where the characteristic patterns are assumed to have either parametric or nonparametric distributions, which structure the null and alternative hypotheses. If there is more than one possible cause to any event at the population level, then Concept 5 states that it is possible to divide these causes into the presumed nonrandom cause of interest (the alternative hypothesis) and all other, presumably random, causes (the null hypothesis). Concept 6 states that if the number representing the outcome of the comparison of the null vs. alternative hypothesis represents the signal in statistical inference formulas, then a measure of dispersion represents noise in the formulas.

Concept 7

Since the statistical inference test formulas use sample data to represent the alternative hypothesis portion of the signal, and sometimes noise, then the specific form of each inference formula can vary, depending on the measurement complexity and purpose of the sample data collected.

This chapter first discusses <u>level of measurement</u>. <u>Measurement</u> is the process of numerically describing entities and events. Measurement can vary in precision and accuracy. This variation is presented in four levels. Two of the levels, <u>nominal</u> and <u>ordinal</u>, are nonparametric, and the other two, interval and ratio, are parametric. The choice of which particular inference test to use is determined by which level of measurement is used in collecting the sample data. In other words, <u>the level of measurement determines exactly when and where each descriptive statistic and inference test will be used</u>.

The rules which define the assignment of an appropriate numerical value to an observation determine the level of measurement. The different levels are defined by the naming, ordering, distancing and zeroing properties inherent in the rules. Why do you need to know these rules? <u>Each descriptive and inferential statistical technique is appropriate for data measured at a certain level</u>. Figure 15 defines each level of measurement and shows the descriptive statistics that are appropriate to each level. Descriptive statistics give a brief summary description of sample data, and they supply the numbers that represent the alternative hypothesis and noise in inference tests.

This chapter also discusses two alternative research strategies that help to determine the type of measurement and inference tests used for the sample data; causal research versus correlational research.

POPULATION ASSUMPTIONS UNDERLYING THE LEVELS OF MEASUREMENT	LEVELS OF MEASUREMENT	CHARACTERISTICS OF LEVEL	DESCRIPTIVE STATISTICS APPROPRIATE TO EACH LEVEL
NON PARAMETRIC (NONMETRIC)	**NOMINAL** (LABELING)	**NOMINAL IS:** · QUALITATIVE · CATEGORICAL · DISCRETE	**NOMINAL STATISTICS** FREQUENCY COUNTS PERCENTS MODES RANGES CONTINGENCY COEFFICIENT
NONNORMAL POPULATION ASSUMPTIONS MADE	**ORDINAL** (LABELING PLUS ORDERING)	**ORDINAL IS:** · QUANTITATIVE · CATEGORICAL · DISCRETE	**ORDINAL STATISTICS** RANKS SIGNS MEDIANS INTERQUARTILE RANGES SPEARMAN CORRELATION COEFFICIENT KENDALL CORRELATION COEFFICIENT
PARAMETRIC (METRIC)	**INTERVAL** (LABELING PLUS ORDERING PLUS EQUAL DISTANCE)	**INTERVAL IS:** · QUANTITATIVE · ARBITRARILY CATEGORICAL · CONTINUOUS	**INTERVAL AND RATIO STATISTICS** MEANS VARIANCES STANDARD DEVIATIONS PEARSON CORRELATION COEFFICIENT BETA COEFFICIENT
NORMAL POPULATION ASSUMPTIONS MADE	**RATIO** (LABELING PLUS ORDERING PLUS EQUAL DISTANCE PLUS ABSOLUTE ZERO)	**RATIO IS:** · QUANTITATIVE · ARBITRARILY CATEGORICAL · CONTINUOUS	

FIGURE 15

A. The Nominal Level of Measurement

The simplest level of measurement is the <u>nominal</u> level. The term nominal refers to naming or labeling. <u>At the nominal level, the numeric values serve to merely name or label a category</u>. Labeling allows for a system of <u>mutually exclusive</u> category classification based on qualitative distinctions. As stated in Chapter 4, qualitative distinctions are differentiations of kind, not degree or amount. These qualitative distinctions determine the complete presence or absence of a characteristic. Membership in one category precludes membership in another category. For example, if an individual is registered to vote as a Democrat, he or she cannot be registered as a Republican or Independent.

A <u>nominal scale</u> consists of two or more named categories into which objects, events or individuals are classified. The categories formed from nominal level data are just different, not more or less different. Therefore, there is no adding, subtracting, multiplying, or dividing categories, because these mathematical manipulations require quantitative, more or less differences. What descriptive statistics can be used at this level?

The only descriptive statistics that can be used at this level are those that are based on simple counting, such as frequency distributions, modes, and ranges. A <u>frequency</u> <u>distribution</u> sorts observations into categories, and describes how often observations fall into each category.

For example, you have gathered religious preference information from a group of 90 acquaintances. You assume that a preference for one religion precludes a preference for any other religion. Once they have indicated their preferences, you then count the number of individuals in each religious category. Twenty six indicate a preference for Catholicism, 24 for some form of Protestantism, 17 for Judaism, 14 for Hinduism, and 9 for Islam. You array this data in such a way as to create a bar graph representation of your frequency distribution, as shown in Figure 16. On the vertical (Y) axis, there are numbers representing the range of frequencies possible in the various religious categories. On the horizontal (X) axis there are the categories into which your data are grouped.

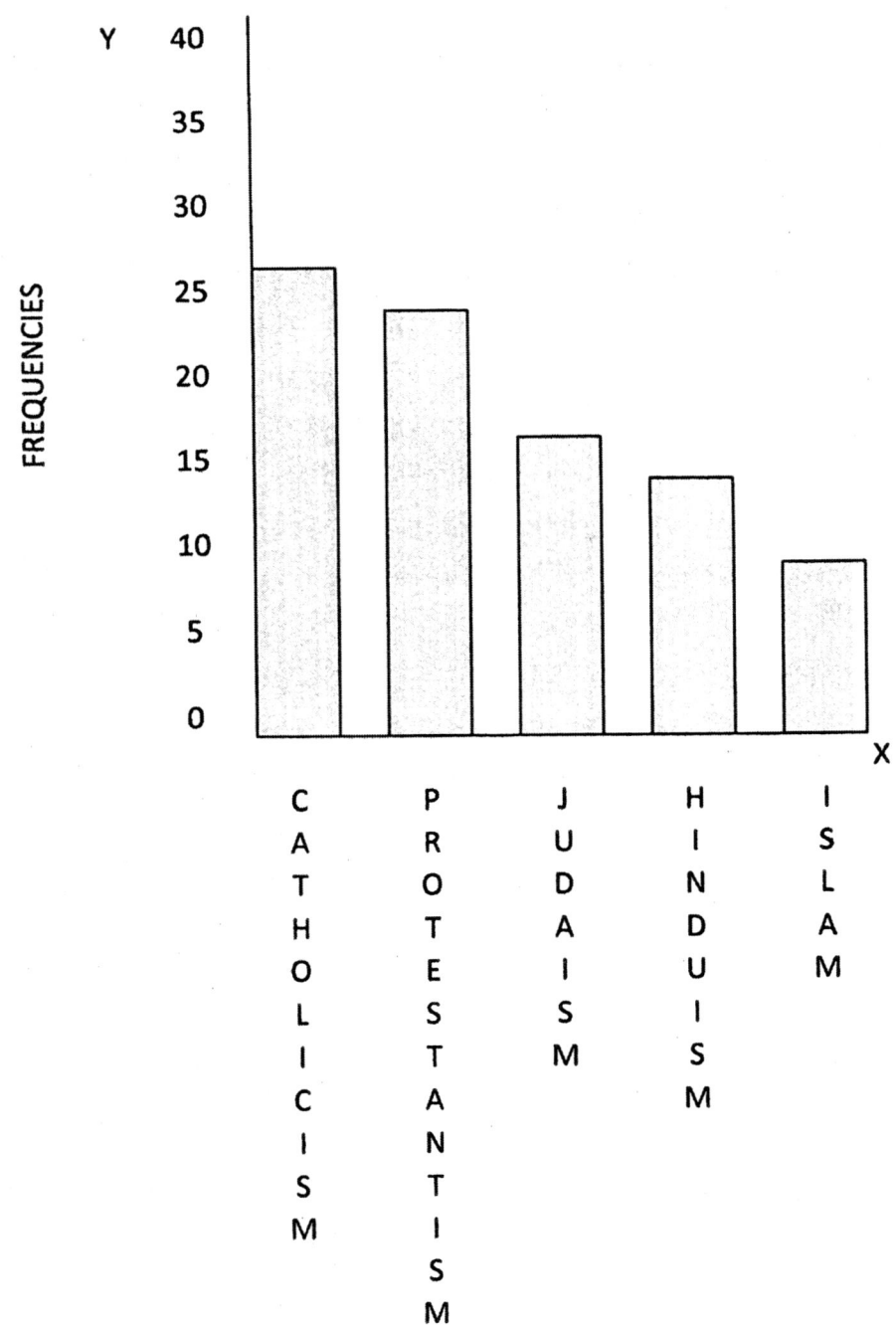

RELIGIOUS CATEGORIES

FIGURE 16

Besides a basic frequency count, researchers can identify a mode and a range in nominal level data. The <u>mode</u> is the most frequently occurring category. In the example the mode is the Catholic category which had 26 observations. If you gave each category a numerical value, from one through five, you could derive the range. The <u>range</u> is a measure of variability that is derived by subtracting the lowest value from the highest value (5-1) and adding one, and it indicates how far apart the highest value is from the lowest value.

Other examples of nominal scales are social security numbers, drivers' license numbers, credit card numbers, and the numbers on sports jersey. In each of these scales the numbers are labels, carrying no more (or less) information than the associated individual names. Arithmetic operations, other than counting, cannot be performed on any of these scales. For example, it would make no sense to subtract one person's sports jersey number from another person's number.

As Figure 15 shows, nominal level variables are qualitative, categorical, and discrete. As mentioned above, a qualitative difference is a difference in kind, not in degree or amount. A category is a qualitative grouping, and an entry into one category cannot be placed in another category. A discrete (or discontinuous) variable has a finite number of distinct and separate categories. In the example of religion there are a finite number of possible categories, although our hypothetical data gathering example certainly did not exhaust all possible religious preferences. At the nominal level no value can fall in between categories. One is either of this religion, or that religion, or no religion.

Can religious categories be ordered in any way? Probably not. Religious preference is analogous to the appreciation of art- a totally subjective experience. There is no agreed upon ordering system for this variable.

The measurement experts conclude that the definitional properties of the nominal level are clear and unambiguous, and that nominal measurement is easily distinguished from ordinal, interval, and ratio measurement. The level of measurement concept becomes somewhat ambiguous at the ordinal level, which is quantitative, not qualitative, but still categorical and discrete.

B. The Ordinal Level of Measurement

Figure 15 indicates that the ordinal level has an additional measurement property. Ordinal measurement continues to label and categorize data, while ordering the data quantitatively. The term ordinal pertains to a succession of magnitude. Ordinal level of measurement is simply but absolutely quantitative. Quantity is the characteristic of an event or entity that permits it to be measured in degree, as more or less, not kind. An ordinal scale defines the relative position of entities or objects with respect to the intensity of a given characteristic. These relative positions are expressed by the algebra of inequalities, as less or more (<, and >, respectively), such that one position in an ordinal scale is never equal to another position. Thus the ordinal level, unlike the nominal level, makes distinctions of more or less, as each category in an ordinal scale is either more than or less than any other category.

Examples of ordinal scales are the order of runners placing in a race, letter grades given in a class, or the ranking of job candidates after interviews. Social class is another example of an ordinal scale. You ask a group of 113 people to indicate which social class they belong to: upper upper, lower upper, upper middle, middle middle, lower middle, upper lower, lower lower. You tell these individuals to use their own subjective definitions of these categories to make their placements. Six define themselves as upper-upper, 11 identify themselves as lower-upper, 34 as upper-middle, 31 as middle-middle, 14 as lower-middle, 11 as upper-lower, and 8 as lower-lower. Figure 17 shows the bar graph representation of the frequency count of responses in each category, which is the same descriptive tool we used in the religious preference example.

In addition to labeling, the ordinal level adds another useful characteristic, ordering. There is an intuitive agreed upon ranking system inherent in the social class example, a fixed order of categories. Most people would agree that somehow upper upper is "more than" lower upper, which is "more than" upper middle, and so on.

Though the categories are ordered, nothing is said about the distance between the categories; in the example the distinctions between social classes are not objectively defined. An ordinal scale is like an elastic tape measure that is stretched unevenly over the measured events or objects. Since the quantitative (more or less) distinctions are not precisely defined, ordinal scales, like nominal scales, do not have the numerical properties necessary for arithmetic operations; no adding, subtracting, multiplying, or dividing can be done with values at the ordinal level.

What descriptive statistics are appropriate to the ordinal level? The seven social classes in our example could be ranked from one (upper upper) to seven (lower lower) and listed in that order, as they are in Figure 17. These ranks become the ordinal level descriptive statistics that are used to describe the sample because the frequencies in each category are compared <u>according to their rank number</u>.

The ranks are the numbers used in ordinal level inference tests. Another ordinal level measure is the <u>median</u>. The median is the rank at which half of the sample respondents fall below and half of the respondents fall above.

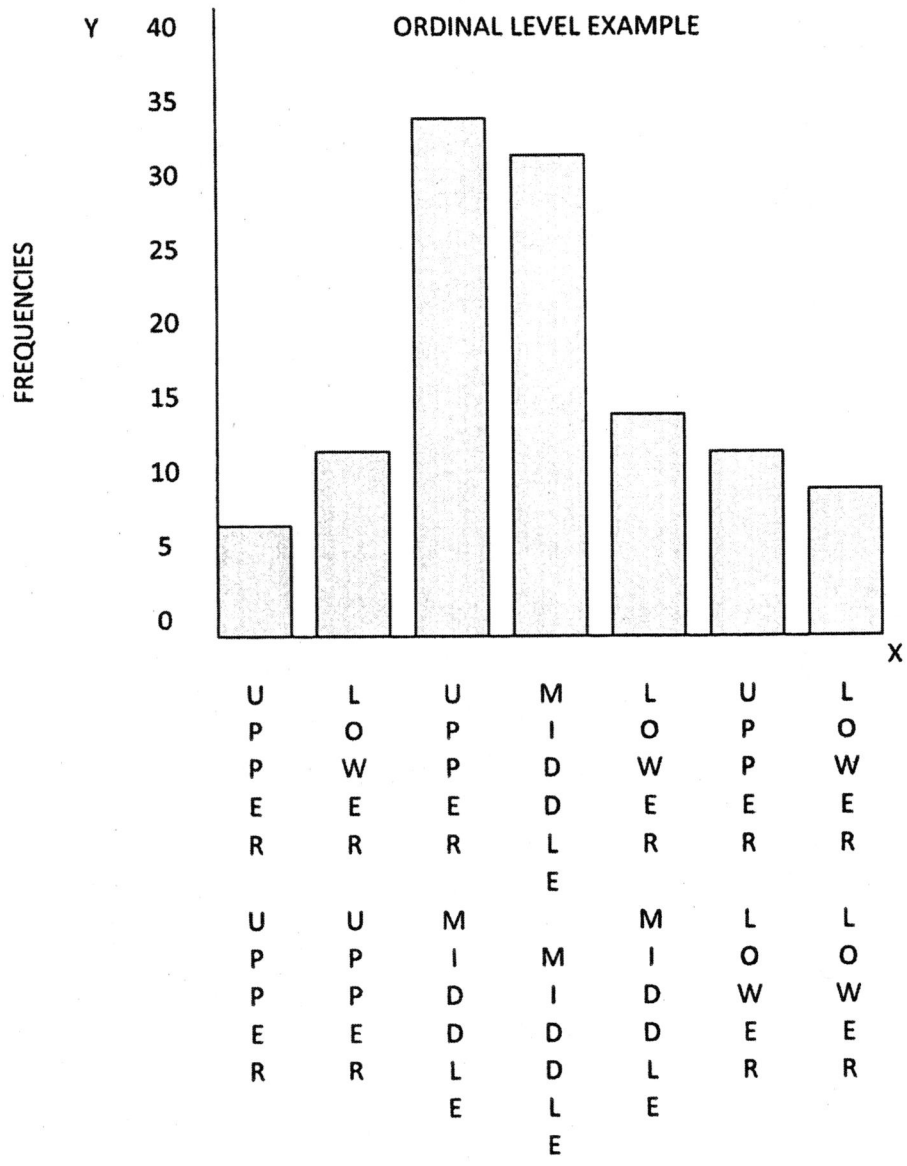

FIGURE 17

Ordinal measurement, unlike nominal measurement, is based on continuous, rather than discrete, data. A <u>continuum</u> is defined as "a continuous extent, succession, or whole, no part of which can be distinguished from neighboring parts except by arbitrary division". A measurement unit from one part of a continuum is no different from a unit from another part of the continuum. An important characteristic of continua from a statistical viewpoint is their infinite divisibility. This means that units on a continuum can be infinitely small or infinitely big. Height, for example, can be measured in any units from millimeters (or smaller) to meters (or bigger). As the definition indicates, unit boundaries on a continuum are arbitrary, since the continuum can be divided in an infinite number of ways.

Ordinal scale examples mentioned were social class, placement in a race, letter grades in a class, and job placement ranks. In each of these examples the underlying measurement dimension is continuous: social class distinctions are presumably based on income, race placements on time, letter grades on points and job rankings on performance scores. Income, time, points and performance scores can be infinitely divided into smaller or larger units.

If ordinal scales are ultimately based on continuums, why is ordinal measurement considered categorical and discrete? Because ordinal scales do not precisely measure intervals between scale units, the measured phenomenon <u>become</u> categorical and discrete, rather than continuous.

When you read in the newspaper about the results from a 10 kilometer race that some of your friends ran in, you find out who placed first and second and so on. The particular article doesn't report the time of the winning runner, or any of the other runners. It may be that the winner barely beat the second place runner, but the third place finisher was far behind the first two. The fourth place runner was even further behind the third, but the fifth was very close to the fourth. Like many fans, maybe you are just interested in the rankings, not the specific times that led to the rankings.

The rankings take on the characteristics of discrete categories. Ordinal scales do not directly measure continua, but simply rank order the continuous information into discrete categories. Crucial continuous level information (such as the times leading to the rank in the 10K race) is lost in this categorization process. And, since the underlying continuum is not explicitly measured, standardized intervals between categories are not established. Therefore ordinal scales, along with nominal scales, are classified as nonparametric, because the underlying continuums are not directly measured.

C. The Interval Level of Measurement

Interval measurement does not leave out the continuum information. The <u>interval</u> level of measurement names and orders categories, <u>retaining the properties of the nominal and ordinal levels, and defines the distance between values in terms of fixed and equal units</u>. An interval scale is an ordered scale with equal intervals everywhere along the scale.

Interval measurement takes place on continuous variables which have equally spaced intervals. Temperature, as measured by either the Fahrenheit or Centigrade scales, is a good example. The distance between degrees when measuring heat is the same at either end of scale, or anywhere along the scale. The difference in heat between 1 and 2 degrees Fahrenheit is the same as the difference between 99 and 100 degrees Fahrenheit.

Standardized, equally spaced intervals from continuous variables allow for the creation of descriptive statistics that cannot be created from data gathered at the nominal and ordinal levels. These descriptive statistics are the mean, variance, and the standard deviation. The formula for the mean is X bar = the sum of all Xs divided by N. X bar is the symbol for the sample mean, X is the numeric coded value of each observation, N is the number of cases or observations. The formula indicates that the mean is an average. An average could fall on a value that does not actually exist in the frequency distribution of sample values that were used to create the average. For example, the average height of a sample of heights could be 68 and 1/2 inches, even though no one in the sample is 68 and 1/2 inches tall. In spite of this, the average height makes sense because height is a continuous variable that can be infinitely divided, with arbitrary interval boundaries.

The mean, like the mode and the median, is a measure of what is known as <u>central tendency</u>. When data are collected and a frequency distribution made, researchers notice that most of the data values cluster in the center of the distribution, and that some of the values tend to be away from the center on either side of the center. This tendency for some values to be away from the center is known as <u>dispersion</u>. The <u>standard deviation</u> is a measure of dispersion that is related to the mean. And like the mean, it is only created from data gathered at the interval and ratio levels of measurement.

In the formulas for the mean and the standard deviation, N is a component in the divisor in both formulas. <u>This indicates that both the mean and the standard deviation are average descriptive statistics</u>. The mean is an average measure of central tendency, and the standard deviation is an average measure of variability, or dispersal from the mean. One of the purposes of the standard deviation is to provide a uniform measure of the distribution of different interval level variables, so that the variables can be compared. Together, the use of means and SDs allows researchers to overcome the "apples/oranges" problem associated with differing measurement scales. Two variables with different measurement scales (e.g., height in inches and weight in pounds) can be compared statistically using means and SDs as long as both variables are at the interval or ratio levels.

The addition of standardized distance interval measurement is important because it allows for addition, subtraction, multiplication, and division. Using the ordinal scale example from the last chapter, you notice that the newspaper report on the 10 kilometer race gave times as well as ranks. The first place runner finished in 29 minutes, 45 seconds, second place in 29'55", third in 34'15", fourth in 34'20", fifth in 39'16", and sixth in 41'44", and so on. You now have the information you need to create a mean and standard deviation, because time is standardized into equal distance intervals.

D. The Ratio Level of Measurement.

What is not known when using interval measurement is exactly what one interval represents in terms of the quality being measured, because interval scales use arbitrary numbers as anchor points on continua. It is never clear exactly how much quantity is reflected by any given number on the scale.

POPULATION ASSUMPTIONS UNDERLYING THE LEVELS OF MEASUREMENT	LEVELS OF MEASUREMENT	DESCRIPTIVE STATISTICS APPROPRIATE TO EACH LEVEL	CAUSAL INFERENCE TESTS APPROPRIATE TO EACH LEVEL	CORRELATIONAL AND REGRESSION TESTS APPROPRIATE TO EACH LEVEL
NON PARAMETRIC (NONMETRIC)	NOMINAL (LABELING)	NOMINAL STATISTICS FREQUENCY COUNTS PERCENTS MODES RANGES CONTINGENCY COEFFICIENT	NOMINAL TESTS BINOMIAL TEST CHI SQUARE GOODNESS OF FIT McNEMAR CHANGES TEST FISHER PROBABILITY TEST CHI SQUARE TEST OF INDEPENDENCE COCHRAN Q TEST	NOMINAL TESTS CRAMER'S V COEFFICIENT TEST
NONNORMAL POPULATION ASSUMPTIONS MADE	ORDINAL (LABELING PLUS ORDERING)	ORDINAL STATISTICS RANKS SIGNS MEDIANS INTERQUARTILE RANGES SPEARMAN CORRELATION COEFFICIENT KENDALL CORRELATION COEFFICIENT	ORDINAL TESTS SIGN TEST WILCOXON SIGNED RANK TEST MEDIAN TEST MANN WHITNEY U TEST KS TWO SAMPLE TEST TEST OF EXTREME REACTIONS KW ONE WAY ANOVA FRIEDMAN TWO WAY ANOVA	ORDINAL TESTS SPEARMAN RANK TEST KENDALL RANK TEST KENDALL PARTIAL RANK TEST KENDALL CONCORDANCE TEST
PARAMETRIC (METRIC)	INTERVAL (LABELING PLUS ORDERING PLUS EQUAL DISTANCE)	INTERVAL AND RATIO STATISTICS MEANS VARIANCES STANDARD DEVIATIONS PEARSON CORRELATION COEFFICIENT BETA COEFFICIENT	INTERVAL AND RATIO TESTS Z TEST ONE SAMPLE T TEST INDEPENDENT T TEST DEPENDENT T TEST F TESTS	INTERVAL AND RATIO TESTS PEARSON CORRELATION TEST T TEST OF BETA COEFFICIENT
NORMAL POPULATION ASSUMPTIONS MADE	RATIO (LABELING PLUS ORDERING PLUS EQUAL DISTANCE PLUS ABSOLUTE ZERO)			

FIGURE 18

In other words, the rules governing interval measurement do not allow for comparisons of proportionate magnitudes, because there is no absolute anchoring or zero point. Thus it is incorrect to say that 80 degrees Fahrenheit is twice the magnitude of 40 degrees Fahrenheit. The ratio level of measurement has all the properties of the previous levels of measurement, with the addition that an absolute zero point is inherently defined by the measurement scheme. Ratio measurement comes from continua where the value of zero represents the absence of a quality, and therefore the absence of quantity. The Kelvin temperature scale is an example of ratio measurement, since zero on the Kelvin scale represents the absolute absence of thermal energy (heat).Since there is an absolute anchor point ratios between quantities can be expressed. Height and weight are ratio scales, because it is possible to conceive of the absolute absence of height and weight. This level of measurement is common in physical variable measurement but it is not common in social science research. Measurement experts state that none of the measurement techniques in social science use ratio scales, except for some of the psychophysical measures, such as reaction time. However, since no statistical inference tests require ratio level properties, all descriptive statistics and inference tests applicable for interval level measurement can be used at the ratio level. The interval and ratio levels of measurement are both directly based on continuums, and therefore fall into the parametric category, as indicated in Figure 18.

E. The exact fit between specific descriptive statistical numbers and specific statistical inference tests.

As Figure 18 indicates, there is a specific correspondence between level of measurement, descriptive statistics and inference tests. Each level of measurement produces its own descriptive statistics which go into inference tests that are specifically tailored for that level of measurement.

To review, at the nominal level you can calculate frequency distributions, modes, and ranges. At the ordinal level you can compute all of the above plus ranks and medians. At the interval and ratio levels you can compute all of the above plus means, variances, and standard deviations. However, the rules of measurement do not allow you to go the other way. You cannot create means, variances and standard deviations for ordinal level variables, and you cannot create ranks and medians at the nominal level of measurement.

Figure 18 demonstrates that sample derived descriptive statistics provide the numerical information for inference test formulas. More specifically, the descriptive statistics relevant to a particular level of measurement are only used in the inference tests appropriate to that level of measurement. For example, frequency counts are the only descriptive statistics that are used in the chi square formula, and means and standard deviations are the only descriptive statistics used in the Z test.

F. Further qualification on testing the alternative hypothesis: Correlation vs. Causality.

Level of measurement variation means that the exact form of inference test formulas used for testing alternative hypotheses varies. Another factor that causes variation in the inference test form is the purpose of measurement, which is indicated in the choice of research design. There are two basic types of research design: one of which attempts to establish correlation, and the other to establish causality. Further understanding of the various formulas that test the alternative hypothesis requires discussion of the distinction between correlation and causal research. Once this distinction is clarified the non-directional and directional forms of the alternative hypothesis can be introduced and defined.

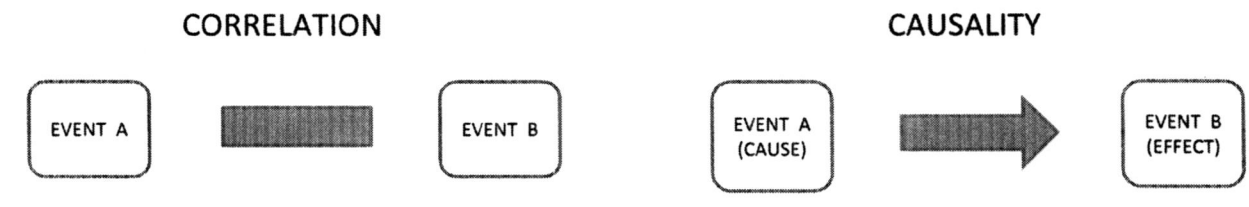

CORRELATION

EVENT A   EVENT B

CORRELATION IS ESTABLISHED WITH NONEXPERIMENTAL RESEARCH WHICH IS BASED ON A NONDIRECTIONAL (TWO WAY) ALTERNATIVE HYPOTHESIS

CAUSALITY

EVENT A (CAUSE)   EVENT B (EFFECT)

CAUSALITY IS ESTABLISHED WITH THE EXPERIMENTAL METHOD; AND EXPERIMENTS ARE OFTEN BASED ON A DIRECTIONAL (ONE WAY) ALTERNATIVE HYPOTHESIS

FIGURE 19

Scientific research applies inductive logic to the process of observation, and then examines the observations to see if the results do or do not support a particular hypothesis. Science is not, however, the only source of questions and answers about the nature of various universes. Religion, philosophy, art and culture are alternative human endeavors undertaken to increase universal understanding. What is unique about science? The methodology of investigation in science is the only form of human endeavor where variables are <u>operationally defined</u> and variable conditions are compared as exactly as possible. This methodology is known as the <u>experimental method</u>.

The experimental method attempts to ascertain causality by establishing a clear linkage between one event and another event. Investigations of causality attempt to establish which event is the antecedent (cause) and which is the consequence (effect), as shown in Figure 19. Establishing causality links events sequentially, in both space and time.

What if researchers are unable to state which way the arrow of causality goes (from A to B, or from B to A)? Is a linkage without a causal arrow adequate for scientific research? A non-causal linkage, also demonstrated in Figure 19, between two events is called a <u>correlation</u>. A non-causal linkage is not enough to establish causality: researchers must have both the link and directional arrow for causality. An experiment attempts to establish causality-both a linkage and a directional arrow. Non-experimental research attempts to establish correlation- a linkage only.

Is correlational research worth doing? Yes, for two reasons. First, correlation research is often the first step in the search for causality. Correlation research can establish which links are plausible for directional arrows. Correlation research can eliminate alternative hypotheses that are not worth testing with experimentation. If a correlation is not established, there is no linkage worth testing further. Second, there are many issues that do not lend themselves to experimentation. Either the issues cannot be studied in laboratory environments or experimentation would be unethical. Many organizational and social policy decisions are made on the basis of correlational research only.

The distinction between causality and correlation allows us to more specifically define the alternative hypothesis. Causal research is usually associated with a directional alternative hypothesis. A <u>directional</u> alternative hypothesis states not only that A causes B, but that A will increase (or decrease) B. A <u>non-directional</u> alternative hypothesis states either that there is simply a non-causal linkage between A and B, or that A has an effect on B, but the exact effect is unknown.

The two types of research each have their own families of statistical inference tests (formulas) within each level of measurement, and the primer presents these families separately when discussing the inference tests for each level of measurement. As we will see in Chapter 11, defining the level of measurement and the research as either causal or correlational are two of the key steps in the statistical decision tree.

Chapter Summary

Level of measurement and the causality-correlation distinction essentially function as categorizers in the hypothesis testing, sample to population inference process. As we shall see in Chapter 8, The specific level of measurement and the choice of causal or correlational research design do not alter the basic inference test formula, nor do they alter how all inference tests are processed.

Section 2:

Level of Measurement and Inferential Statistical Formulas

This section of the book, Chapters 8, 9 and 10, presents some inference tests usually presented in an introductory course. They will be discussed according to the appropriate level of measurement. Chapter 8 presents a six step processing model that is applicable to all inference tests, regardless of measurement level or the type of research design utilized. Chapter 9 presents four of the inference tests, two causal and two correlational, used at the nominal and ordinal measurement levels, and Chapter 10 presents a series of five closely related interval/ratio causal inference tests and a single correlational test.

The purpose in presenting these inference tests is to demonstrate how the seven concepts presented in Chapters 1 through 7 will help you understand the inferential statistics portion of your introductory course. In the chapters of this section the emphasis is on the similarities among all the inference tests, rather than the differences between them.

Chapter 8:

The Six Step Processing Model Appropriate to All Inference Tests

<u>Chapter Outline</u>

Chapter Preview

    A. The Six Step Model

    – Step 1

    – Step 2

    – Step 3

    – Step 4

    – Step 5

    – Step 6

<u>Chapter Summary</u>

Chapter Preview

This chapter will present a six step model that is used in <u>all</u> statistical infer-ence tests. The six steps are: 1) determine the level of measurement; 2) derive the relevant descriptive statistics from the sample data; 3) put the descriptive statistics in the appropriate slots in the appropriate inference test formulas; 4) derive the formula number; 5) compare the formula derived number to the appropriate table number; 6) if the formula number is larger (usually) than the table number at the selected alpha level, reject the null hypothesis and accept the alternative hypothesis. If the formula number is equal to or smaller than the table number, retain the null hypothesis and reject the alternative hypothesis.

A. The Six Step Model

As introductory statistics courses move from one inference test formula to another, a fundamental formula commonality is not usually emphasized by the authors of the assigned textbooks: <u>Every statistical inference test formula follows the same six step procedure</u>. This is very unfortunate because a con-ceptual understanding of the purpose of inferential statistics is enhanced by understanding that, although inference test formulas can look quite dif-ferent, they all follow the same sequence aimed at the same ultimate goal, which is to probabilistically test the alternative versus the null hypotheses.

Step 1: **Determine the level of measurement.**

The <u>first</u> step is to determine the level of measurement used in the sample data collection. This is often done by the researcher before the data collection occurs, and, if it is not, it must be assessed after the data are collected and before data analysis begins. The important point is that this step is a choice made by the researcher; it cannot be incorporated into a statistical software program. The following example, shown in Figure 20, will be followed through the six steps.

You are a purchaser for a sporting goods store. You want to know if there is any relation between season of the year and the purchase of basketballs. Since you are only interested in two discrete categorical outcomes (each basketball was sold or not sold), you determine that you will be using the nominal level of measurement.

THE 6 STEP PROCESSING MODEL APPLICABLE TO ALL INFERENCE TESTS

STEP 1	STEP 2	STEP 3	STEP 4	STEP 5	STEP 6
DETERMINE THE LEVEL OF MEASUREMENT OF THE SAMPLE DATA	CALCULATE DESCRIPTIVE STATISTICS FROM SAMPLE DATA	PUT THE DESCRIPTIVE STATISTICS INTO THE INFERENCE TEST FORMULA	COMPUTE THE FORMULA NUMBER	COMPARE THE FORMULA AND TABLE NUMBERS	REJECT OR RETAIN THE NULL

EXAMPLE:

STEP 1	STEP 2	STEP 3	STEP 4	STEP 5	STEP 6
NOMINAL LEVEL	SALES 30 BALLS 45 BALLS 20 BALLS 5 BALLS	$\chi^2 = \sum \frac{(O - E)^2}{E}$ $\frac{(30 - 25)^2}{25}$ + $\frac{(45 - 25)^2}{25}$ + $\frac{(20 - 25)^2}{25}$ + $\frac{(5 - 25)^2}{25}$	FORMULA NUMBER IS 34.00	THE FORMULA NUMBER, 34.00, IS BIGGER THAN THE TABLE NUMBER, 7.82	THE NULL HYPOTHESIS THAT THERE IS NO RELATION BETWEEN BASKETBALL SALES AND SEASONS IS REJECTED, AND THE ALTERNATIVE THAT THERE IS A RELATIONSHIP IS ACCEPTED.

FIGURE 20

Step 2: **Derive the descriptive statistics**

The <u>second</u> step involves the selection of which descriptive statistics should be generated from the sample data. This step follows from the measurement level choice because each descriptive statistic is only appropriate to certain measurement levels. Since descriptive statistics are a necessary component of inference test formulas, they must be generated before the formulas can be used.

You count the number of basketballs sold over the four seasons in the last calendar year. You come up with the frequency counts shown in Step 2 of Figure 20: 30 balls sold in the fall, 45 in the winter, 20 in the spring, and 5 in the summer.

Step 3: **Put the descriptive statistics into the statistical inference formula**

The <u>third</u> step requires the placement of the selected descriptive statistics into the sample data slots in the inference tests appropriate to the chosen measurement level. This step is necessary before proceeding to the fourth step, which is to actually work the formula.

In the example the null hypothesis is that there is no relation between season and basketball sales, while the alternative hypothesis states that a relation exists between season and sales. If the null hypothesis were true you would expect on a random basis approximately the same number of balls to be sold in each season. The appropriate formula to determine whether season and basketball sales are related is the chi square test, shown in Step 3 of Figure 20.

Given that you sold 100 balls during the year, the null hypothesis suggests that you should have sold 25 balls during each season. In the chi square formula the null hypothesis is represented by the <u>expected</u> frequencies, 25 for each season. Your <u>observed</u> frequencies, 30 balls sold in the fall, 45 in winter, 20 in spring, and 5 in summer, represent the alternative hypothesis.

Step 4: **Compute the formula number**

In the <u>fourth</u> step a number is calculated by correctly manipulating the formula. In the example the chi square formula is repeated four times, once for each of the four seasons. Σ, the summation sign in the formula means that you add together the computations of the formula applied to each season. In our example the summed formula number is 34. As we shall see in Step 5, bigger formula numbers generally indicates that the data support the alternative hypothesis, while smaller formula numbers typically suggest the results support the null hypothesis.

Step 5: **Compare the formula number to the table number**

In this step the formula number derived in step 4 is compared to the appropriate inference test table usually shown in the back of statistics textbooks. As stated earlier, every inference test is connected with an assumed randomly occurring distribution whose values can be placed in a statistical table. For every inference test formula that is presented in a statistics textbook, there is a corresponding statistical table in the back of that book. Which table number the formula derived number is compared with usually depends on sample size and the alpha level chosen.

CRITICAL VALUES OF CHI-SQUARE

df	LEVEL OF SIGNIFICANCE					
	0.20	0.10	0.05	0.02	0.01	0.001
1	1.64	2.71	3.84	5.41	6.63	10.83
2	3.22	4.61	5.99	7.82	9.21	13.82
3	4.64	6.25	7.82	9.84	11.34	16.27
4	5.99	7.78	9.49	11.67	13.28	18.46
5	7.29	9.24	11.07	13.39	15.09	20.52
6	8.56	10.64	12.59	15.03	16.81	22.46
7	9.80	12.02	14.07	16.62	18.48	24.32
8	11.03	13.36	15.51	18.17	20.09	26.12
9	12.24	14.68	16.92	19.68	21.67	27.88
10	13.44	15.99	18.31	21.16	23.21	29.59
11	14.63	17.28	19.68	22.62	24.72	31.26
12	15.81	18.55	21.03	24.05	26.22	32.91
13	16.98	19.81	22.36	25.47	27.69	34.53
14	18.15	21.06	23.68	26.87	29.14	36.12
15	19.31	22.31	25.00	28.26	30.58	37.70
16	20.46	23.54	26.30	29.63	32.00	39.25
17	21.62	24.77	27.59	31.00	33.41	40.79
18	22.76	25.99	28.87	32.35	34.81	42.31
19	23.90	27.20	30.14	33.69	36.19	43.82
20	25.04	28.41	31.41	35.02	37.57	45.32
21	26.17	29.62	32.67	36.34	38.93	46.80
22	27.30	30.81	33.92	37.66	40.29	48.27
23	28.43	32.01	35.17	38.97	41.64	49.73
24	29.55	33.20	36.42	40.27	42.98	51.18
25	30.68	34.38	37.65	41.57	44.31	52.62
26	31.80	35.56	38.89	42.86	45.64	54.05
27	32.91	36.74	40.11	44.14	46.96	55.48
28	34.03	37.92	41.34	45.42	48.28	56.89
29	35.14	39.09	42.56	46.69	49.59	58.30
30	36.25	40.26	43.77	47.96	50.89	59.70

FIGURE 21

Figure 21 presents the table relevant to our example. It is a chi square table of <u>critical values</u> that one would find in the back of most statistic textbooks. The numbers in the table represent the hurdles that must be overcome to reject the null hypothesis. To identify the appropriate hurdle, you must first choose an alpha level (level of significance) and determine your degrees of freedom. <u>Degrees of freedom</u> for the chi square test are the number of comparisons (the number of times the formula is repeated to derive a formula number) minus one. In the season/basketball example the number of comparisons is four: subtract one and you have three degrees of freedom. Choosing an alpha level of .05, the critical value or "hurdle" for 3 degrees of freedom is 7.82. You then compare 34, your formula number, to 7.82, your table number, and see that the formula number is bigger and therefore hurdles over the table number.

Step 6. **Reject or retain the null hypothesis**

In the <u>sixth</u> step, the probability statement derived from the comparison of the formula number to the appropriate table number is now compared to the alpha level probability to determine if the null or the alternative hypothesis should be rejected. This step cannot be automated; this decision is made by actually examining at the results of the data analysis.

If the formula number is bigger than the appropriate table number, you may reject the null hypothesis and accept the alternative hypothesis. The example data show a relation between seasons and basketball sales at the population level. If the example data were different, and the formula number was smaller than 7.82, then the decision would be different. You would reject the alternative hypothesis and retain the null hypothesis.

Chapter Summary

In the olden days before computers all six steps were done manually. Now Steps 2 through 5 are automated because they are incorporated into statistical software programs, which means that they can be done by a computer once sample data are entered, the level of measurement of the data is determined, and then the computer is told which inference formula will be used to analyze the data and test the alternative versus the null hypothesis. After the analysis is done (Steps 2 through 5) the programs will provide printouts of the results of the formula and table number comparison, including the particular probability statement that results from the comparison. Comparing the formula-derived probability statement to the alpha level probability statement allows researchers to make decisions regarding the alternative versus null hypotheses.

Chapter 9:

Nonparametric Causal and Correlational Inference Tests

Chapter Outline

Chapter Preview

    A. A Nominal Causal Inference Test Formula: Chi Square

    B. A Nominal Correlation Coefficient Formula: Cramer's V

    C. An Ordinal Causal Inference Test: Mann-Whitney U

    D. An Ordinal Correlation Coefficient Formula: Spearman

Chapter Summary

Chapter Preview

The nominal and ordinal levels of measurement are nonparametric. The nominal level causal test that is presented is <u>chi square</u>, utilized in Chapter 8 in the 6-step processing model example. <u>Cramer's V</u>, a nominal level correlation coefficient, is also presented. At the ordinal level, the <u>Mann-Whitney U</u>

test is presented as the causal inference test, and the <u>Spearman rank order</u> correlation coefficient is presented as the correlation inference test.

The variable populations measured at the ordinal and nominal levels do not have normal parametric distribution characteristics. Despite the lack of an assumed normal distribution, inferences from samples to populations can be made from data gathered at the nominal and ordinal levels. If nominal and ordinal tests infer from samples to populations, then everything said about the null versus the alternative hypothesis applies at these two levels. Nominal and ordinal measurement levels have both causal and correlational inference tests (tests of the strength of a relation between variables).

A. A nominal causal inference test formula: chi square

The chi square inference test was used in the example of the six step processing model presented in Chapter 8. The descriptives that go into the chi square formula come from contingency tables of frequency counts formed into categories. A contingency table is a joint frequency distribution of observations, as defined by the discrete categories of one or more variables. Figure 22 presents an example of a two variable contingency table, where the frequency counts have been converted to percentages.

	DEMOCRAT	REPUBLICAN
FEMALE	55%	45%
MALE	45%	55%

FIGURE 22

From this table many nominal level inference tests can be computed, the most common of which is chi square. The chi square test tells us the likelihood that the two variables, gender and political affiliation, are statistically independent. Statistical independence would support the null hypothesis, which says that there is no relation between the two variables. Chi square tests the null hypothesis that the observed joint distribution of cases would have happened by chance, where no association exists between the two variables in the population, versus the alternative hypothesis, that the observed reflect an association between gender and political affiliation.

Examination of Figure 23 indicates that the numbers in the chi square formula are based on frequency counts. Since this is the nominal level of measurement, no means, variances, or standard deviations are used in any of the nominal level formulas, including chi square. In chi square the expected score, representing the null hypothesis, is subtracted from the observed score, representing the alternative hypothesis. The expected score is the score that is expected if there is no relation between the variables. The observed scores are the frequency counts found in the actual sample data.

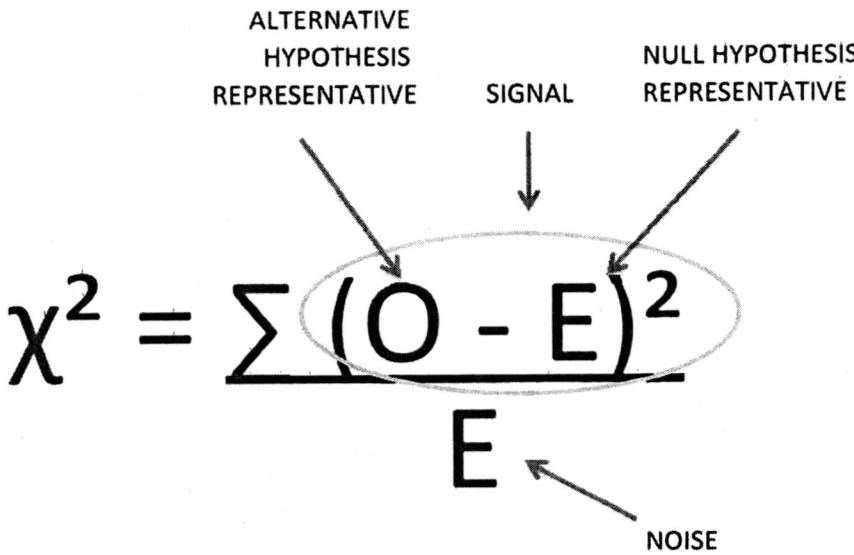

CHI SQUARE FORMULA

FIGURE 23

The signal in chi square is formed by subtracting the null representative (expected score) from the alternative representative (observed score). The denominator in chi square, shown in Figure 23, uses the expected scores as the "noise" factor. Expected scores represent noise only in the sense that they represent the null hypothesis, thus giving the null hypothesis (randomness) the usual second opportunity to decrease the signal quality of the number representing the alternative hypothesis.

B. A nominal correlation inference formula: Cramer's V

The chi square formula presented in Figure 23 does not indicate the intensity or strength of association between two variables. The Cramer's V coefficient presented in Figure 24 measures the strength of association for variables measured at the nominal level. The larger the value of Cramer's V, the stronger the relation between the two variables. In the formula the number generated from the chi square formula is the numerator which signals the outcome of the struggle between the alternative and null hypotheses.

The denominator is composed of N, the sample size, times q, which is the number of rows (minus one) times the number of columns (minus one) in the table. N times q represents noise because the greater the sample size combined with more categories in the data (rows and columns), the greater the likelihood of variability in the data.

NOMINAL LEVEL CORRELATION COEFFICIENT

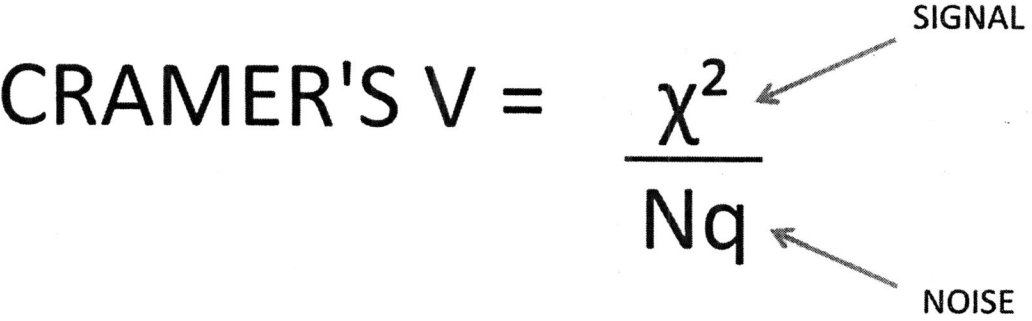

$$\text{CRAMER'S V} = \frac{\chi^2}{Nq}$$

SIGNAL

NOISE

FIGURE 24

C. An ordinal causal inference test.

One ordinal level causal inference test is the Mann-Whitney U test, shown in Figure 25. This test compares the rankings of two different entities or groups. It follows a different pattern for testing the null against the alternative hypothesis.

First, the null hypothesis is stated by giving R the value based on maximum rank mixing between the two groups, which minimizes any potential overall rank differences between the two groups. Then, in a separate application of the formula, the alternative hypothesis, that there is a significant difference in overall ranks between the two groups, is tested by using the actual rank results on one group in the R slot.

ORDINAL LEVEL CAUSAL INFERENCE TEST:
THE MANN-WHITNEY U TEST

$$U = \frac{R - (N)(N + 1)}{2}$$

FIGURE 25

As an example, you are a sports psychologist. You want to demonstrate that a new training technique reduces times in long distance running events. You divide 10 runners into two equal groups. One group gets the new technique, and the other group does not. Your alternative hypothesis is that the five runners in the trained group are all faster than the five runners who did not get the training. To test this alternative hypothesis you add the numbers one through five to get the ranks for the trained group. This number, which is 15, substitutes for R in the formula. Or, as an optional way to test the alternative hypothesis, you could use the untrained group to derive R. In this case you would add 6 + 7 + 8 + 9 + 10, which equals 40.

Subtracted from R is (N)(N+1)/2. In (N)(N+1)/2, N is the number of individuals in the trained group. In our example (N)N+1)/2 also equals 15. Multiplying N by N+1 and dividing by 2 gives the same result as adding one through five. (N)(N+1) is the part of the formula that represents the ideal research results. In our example using the trained group to provide R gives 15, and R-(N)(N+1)/2 equals 15-15, giving a U of zero. If you used the results from the untrained group to provide R, the U would be 25. These results would provide maximum support for your alternative hypothesis, which is that there is the maximum possible difference between the two groups.

However, in order to provide a U that represents the null hypothesis, you hypothetically and maximally mix the results. Hypothetically, you indicate that the runners from the trained group came in 1st, 3rd, 6th, 8th, and 10th. The untrained runners came in 2nd, 4th, 5th, 7th, and 9th. The ranks from the two groups are maximally mixed. To get R for the trained group you add 1, 3, 6, 8, and 10, the numbers representing each of the places of the trained group runners. The result is 28. (N)(N+1)/2 still gives a result of 15. Subtracting 15 from 28 results in a U of 13. This result is maximally supportive of the null hypothesis, the hypothesis of no difference. Similarly, you could add 2, 4, 5, 7 and 9 to get an R for the untrained group of 27. You could subtract 15 from 27 to get a U of 12. In this example, the minimal overall difference between the two groups is shown by the minimal difference in their U scores.

In the example the formula was applied four times, twice to test the alternative hypothesis and twice to test the null hypothesis. This was done to help you understand the process. However, in actual application you would only use one group's results to test the alternative hypothesis, by using the actual rank results of either group in the R slot. Then, in a separate application of the formula, the null is numerically stated by giving R the value based on the maximum rank mixing between the two groups. The second step, testing the null hypothesis, has already been done by statisticians. The results of this testing, done at various sample sizes, are built into the Mann-Whitney U critical values table in the back of many statistics textbooks.

This use of separate applications of the same formula to test the null and alternative hypotheses separately to create a signal is a process that is not unique to the Mann-Whitney U test; it is the standard procedure for ordinal level causal inference tests.

The Mann-Whitney U test and all small sample (25 or less) ordinal causal tests, unlike the chi square and the interval level inference formulas, do not use a denominator in the formulas to represent noise. Ordinal tests deal with noise in a different way. Ordinal tests sometimes use a version of the range, the number of rank values, as the measure of dispersion. The generic ordinal level version of the null hypothesis is that each of the two compared groups of ranks are equally and evenly distributed through all possible ranks. Thus the maximum number of mixed rank values, which in our example yielded an R of 28, represents both the null hypothesis and noise.

Measurement experts realize that the lack of a separate noise correction factor in ordinal level inference tests decreases the accuracy of the inference process. This deficiency is corrected by moving to an inference test with a separate noise correction factor as soon as possible. One way to get to an inference test with a separate noise correction factor is to use a sample with N > 25 for each comparison group, even if the data is collected at the ordinal level.

When the sample size of each compared group becomes greater than 25, ordinal level causal tests shift to the pattern used for nominal and interval/ratio causal tests first demonstrated in Figure 12:

$$\frac{\text{alternative-null}}{\text{noise}} = \frac{\text{signal}}{\text{noise}}$$

This is done by using either a version of the chi square or Z test to replace the ordinal test as the inference test comparing the null and alternative hypotheses, even when the data are collected at the ordinal level of measurement. An explanation of the reasons underlying this shift will be made when the normal distribution is revisited in Chapter 10.

D. An ordinal correlation coefficient: Spearman.

You want to find out if there is any relation between the ranked placements of a single group of runners from two separate races. Figure 26 presents the Spearman correlation coefficient, which is one of several ordinal level correlation formulas that could be used to test for a possible relation. Any correlation formula attempts to numerically measure the degree of association between two variables. In the Spearman formula these two variables are called X and Y. $\sum X$ squared is the sum of the first race ranks squared and $\sum Y$ squared is the sum of the second race ranks squared. Added together they represent the alternative hypothesis. $\sum d$ squared is the sum of difference scores between the X and Y ranks of each individual squared. The greater the sum of the difference scores, the less the association between variables x and y. Since the null hypothesis is that there is no association between X and Y, $\sum d$ squared represents the null hypothesis. Subtracting $\sum d$ squared from $\sum x$ squared+$\sum y$ squared results in the signal, which is the numerator. The numerator is divided by $2\sqrt{(\sum x}$ squared+$\sum y$ squared), the denominator which represents noise.

ORDINAL LEVEL CORRELATION COEFFICIENT:
SPEARMAN

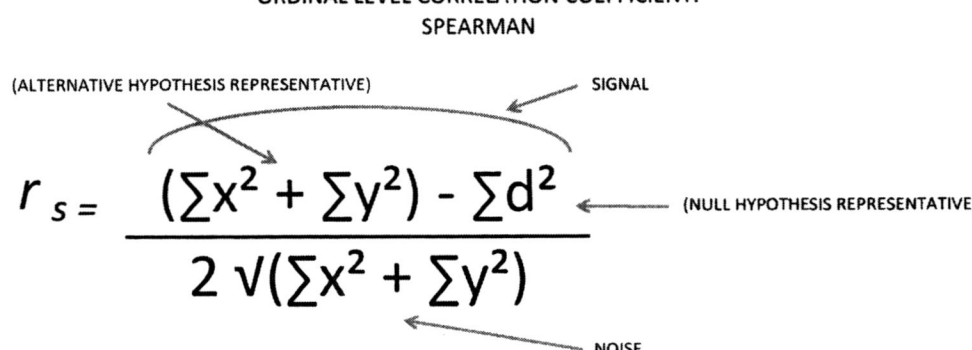

$$r_s = \frac{(\sum x^2 + \sum y^2) - \sum d^2}{2\sqrt{(\sum x^2 + \sum y^2)}}$$

(ALTERNATIVE HYPOTHESIS REPRESENTATIVE)   SIGNAL

(NULL HYPOTHESIS REPRESENTATIVE)

NOISE

FIGURE 26

Chapter Summary

This chapter presented four nonparametric inference tests, two at the nominal level of measurement and two at the ordinal level. The sole purpose of presenting these formulas was to demonstrate their fundamental similarities, despite their superficial differences. Like all inference tests, these four formulas utilize both numerical representatives of the alternative and null hypotheses, creating a signal, and numerical representatives of dispersion or variability, representing noise.

Chapter 10:

Parametric Causal and Correlational Inference Tests

Chapter Summary

Chapter Preview

Chapter 10 continues with the theme of <u>formula similarity</u>, based on the concepts of the alternative versus the null hypothesis (Concept 5) and signal versus noise (Concept 6). The chapter begins with a more specific presentation of the normal parametric distribution that directly or indirectly underlies all interval/ratio inference tests. The chapter starts with the simplest causal inference test and proceeds to more complex formulas, beginning with the Z test formula, continuing through the three t test formulas, and ending with the F test formula. The Pearson correlation coefficient and the t test for regression are presented as the correlation inference tests at the interval/ratio level of measurement. The chapter concludes with a discussion of how the logic of the normal distribution can be used with non-normal variable populations and even with nonparametric events.

A. The Normal Distribution Revisited

The normal distribution will be re-examined more specifically because of its close relation to all interval/ratio inference tests, particularly the Z test. Figure 27 presents the theoretical normal distribution again, this time with a mean and standard deviations (SDs) added. The mean and standard deviations (which can only be created from interval or ratio data) help to define the distribution. In the theoretical normal distribution 34.1 % of the scores will fall between the mean and one SD, and double that percentage, 68.2 %, will occur between one SD below and one SD above the mean. Consequently most observations, a little more than 2/3, will fall around the center of the distribution, from -1 to +1 SD. As we move further from the center in either direction fewer and fewer observations occur. 13.6 % of the scores will occur between the first and second SD, on either side of the mean. If the two percentages are added together, they equal 27.2 %. Adding this number to 68.2% means that going two SDs away from the mean on either side accounts for 95.4 % of the distribution. 2.1 % of the scores occur between two and three SDs from the mean, and this percentage doubled is 4.2 %. Adding this number to 95.4 % indicates that 99.6 % of the distribution is accounted for by going three SDs from the mean on both sides.

Usually normal distributions are graphed to only three SDs on either side of the mean. This gives the appearance that the curve touches the horizontal axis at three standard deviations. This appearance is an illusion, as the theoretical normal distribution never touches the horizontal axis, no matter how many SDs away from the mean. If the curve touched the horizontal axis, it would indicate that the event being studied led to absolute, not probabilistic, outcomes.

THE THEORETICAL (PERFECT) NORMAL DISTRIBUTION

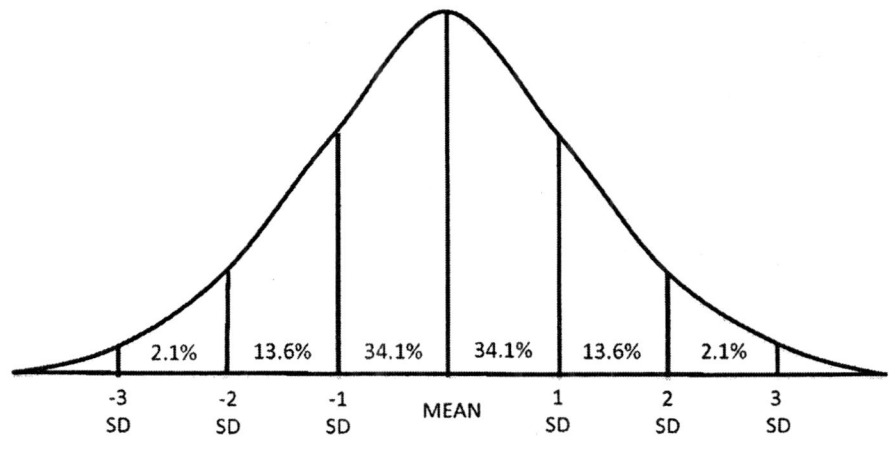

| 2.1% | 13.6% | 34.1% | 34.1% | 13.6% | 2.1% |

-3 SD, -2 SD, -1 SD, MEAN, 1 SD, 2 SD, 3 SD

FIGURE 27

B. In Interval/Ratio Data, the Mean is the Signal and the Standard Deviation is Noise

In statistics noise is either called random error or variability. If variability is noise then variability obscures the signal clarity of a descriptive statistic meant to summarize central tendency, such as a mean.

At the interval or ratio levels of measurement means and standard deviations are used to describe the data. The mean is the signal and the standard deviation is noise. The mean is the signal because it is the number most representative of the approximately normal distribution of data. The mean is the one number best suited to describe the data. What could make the mean a strong (accurate) or weak (inaccurate) representative of the data?

Examine Figures 27, 28, 29 and 30. Figure 27 is the normal, bell shaped distribution. The mean is at the center of the distribution, and the standard deviations on either side of the mean include the percentages of the theoretical distribution discussed above. Now look at the altered "normal" distribution of Figure 28. The center of the distribution is lower and the amount of the distribution under the curve away from the center on either side is higher. This indicates that there is greater variability and larger standard deviations- more scores are further away from the center of the distribution. In Figure 29 the center of the distribution is higher than in the theoretical normal curve, and the number of scores away from the center of the distribution is lower, indicating less variability (smaller standard deviations) away from the center. The scores are all bunched closely around the mean.

Finally, look at Figure 30. <u>All</u> the scores fall exactly in the center; there is no variability away from the center (SD=0). In this figure each score is exactly the same as the mean. Figure 30 demonstrates a situation where every observed value is the same, thus making the mean equate with each raw data value. Referring back to the example used in Chapter 6, this is the numerical analog of everyone running from the ceiling fire at the same moment with the same intensity! In this situation there is only signal, no noise. In Figure 29 almost (but not quite all) of the observed values are on or close to the mean. In this situation the signal is strong but slightly weakened by some noise. Not every value is the same as the mean. To return to the ceiling fire example, it means that some people did not exit the room at exactly the same moment with exactly the same intensity. Some other variables (noise) were affecting their behavior. Nonetheless, they did not vary much in their exiting behavior.

"NORMAL" CURVE WITH LARGE VARIABILITY

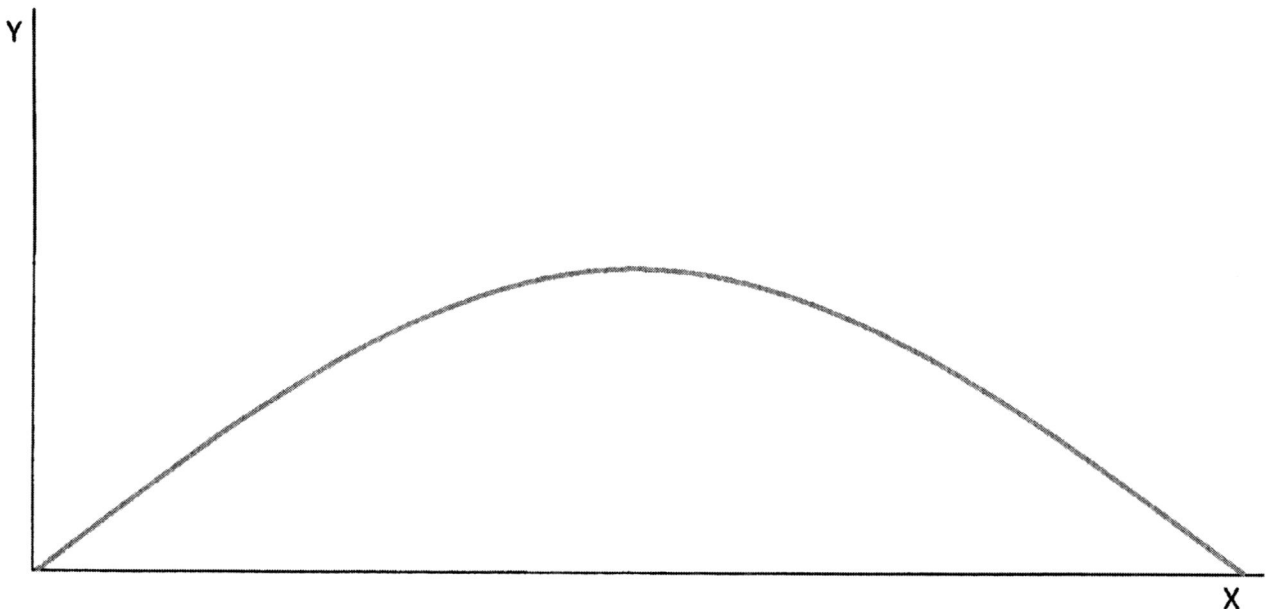

FIGURE 28

Figure 28 demonstrates a situation where many raw values are very far from the mean. The greater this dispersal (variability) is from the mean, the greater the noise, and the weaker the signal. A larger standard deviation (noise) obscures the mean (signal). In the ceiling fire example relevant to Figure 28, some people are hiding under their desks, some are rushing for the door, others are standing around indecisively, and others are trying to put out the fire.

"NORMAL" CURVE WITH SMALL VARIABILITY

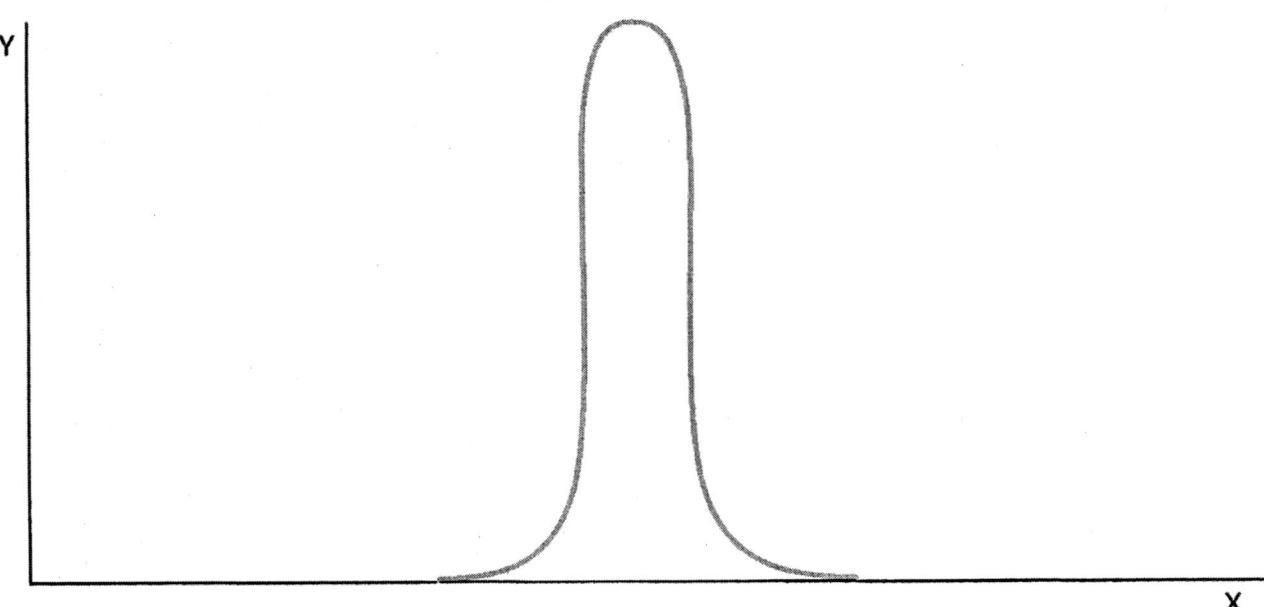

FIGURE 29

To review, the mean, or any summarizing descriptive statistic, is chosen to represent more than itself. With interval/ratio data, the mean is the signal, a number that potentially says something meaningful about the raw data. If the raw data scores are close to the mean (less variability), as in Figures 29 and 30, then the mean is a clear signal that closely resembles all the scores. In Figure 28 there are many raw data scores that are far away from the mean on either side (high variability), and therefore not well represented by the mean. These highly variable scores indicate noise that obscures the clarity of the mean as a signal.

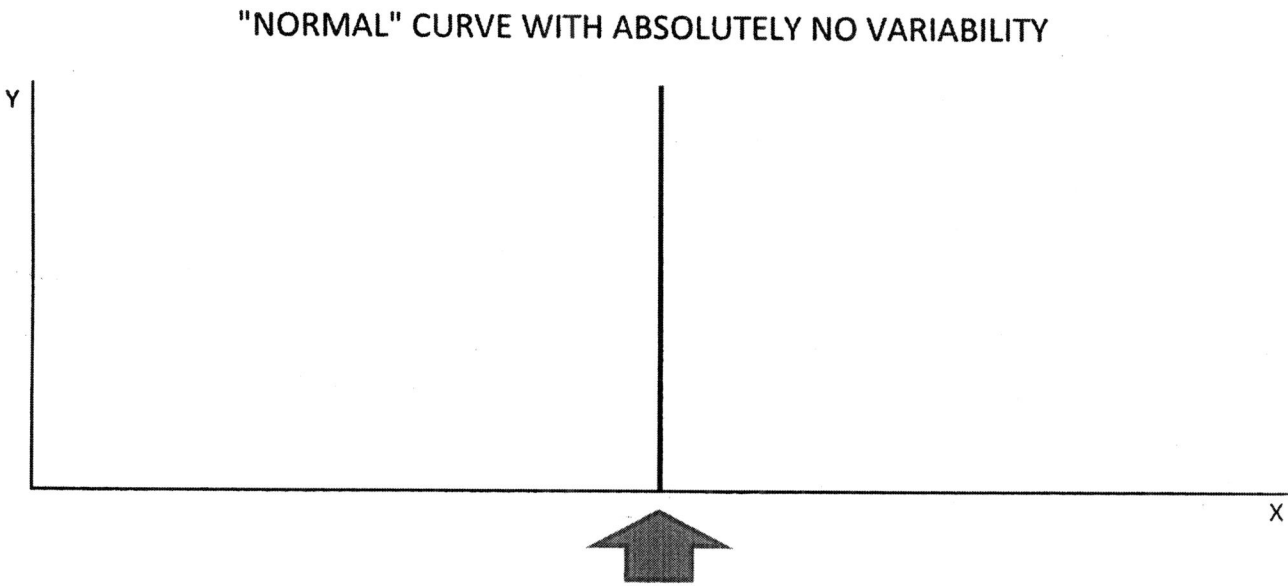

"NORMAL" CURVE WITH ABSOLUTELY NO VARIABILITY

(THIS "CURVE" REPRESENTS ALL X VALUES, AND THE MEAN, MEDIAN, AND MODE OF X; SINCE THERE ARE NO OTHER VALUES OF X, THERE IS NO VARIABILITY)

FIGURE 30

Researchers have two methods for dealing with variability. One method is to exert various forms of control in the research design, before and during the actual study. The second method is to take the noise into account when performing statistical inference tests. This is seen in the basic signal/noise formula (see Figure 31) that was discussed in Chapter 6.

C. Signals, noise, and the causal family of interval/ratio inference tests.

Figure 31, first shown in Chapter 6 as Figure 13, shows the signal/noise formula that is the basic model for all interval/ratio inference tests. To review, in each interval/ratio formula, the signal is the numerator portion of the fraction, and the signal is made clearer by increasing distance between the number representing the alternative hypothesis and the number representing the null hypothesis. Noise is represented by the denominator, and the denominator is the standard deviation, a measure of variability.

BASIC STRUCTURE OF ALL INTERVAL/RATIO FORMULAS:

<u>SIGNAL (ALTERNATIVE - NULL)</u>
NOISE

FIGURE 31

<u>Every</u> interval/ratio statistical inference formula has the same structure: signal (alternative-null)/noise. Each numerator is composed of the sample mean(s) (the alternative hypothesis representative) and the population mean (null hypothesis representative), which is always subtracted from the sample mean(s). Each denominator consists of a standard deviation or variance (the standard deviation squared) corrected by sample size, which reflects noise.

Figure 32 shows the family of related interval/ratio causal inference tests that use this basic structure: the Z test, the one sample t test, the dependent t test, and the independent t test. In each of these formulas, we insert the appropriate descriptive statistics from sample data- means, variances, standard deviations, and sample sizes- to calculate each formula.

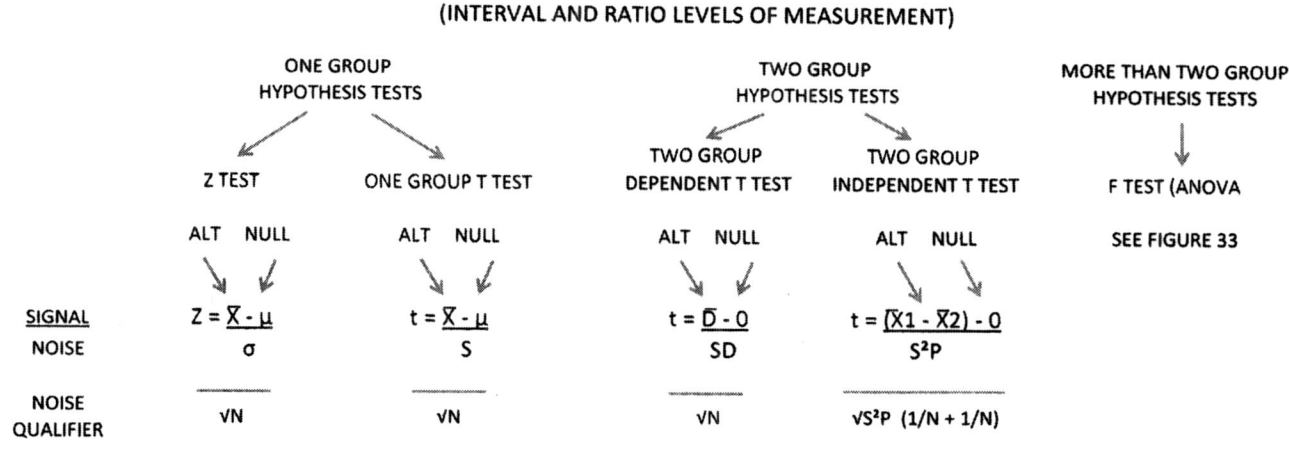

FIGURE 32

Why are the formulas structured this way? A sample mean must pass two tests to be considered a strong signal and demonstrate a statistically significant difference. The sample mean must be big enough to withstand the challenge of the null hypothesis, as represented by subtracting the population mean from the sample mean. If it withstands this challenge it must now face the challenge of noise, as represented by the standard deviation or variance. Dividing the signal (numerator) by the standard deviation (denominator) reduces the size of the formula number, which reduces the possibility of significant results. Since noise exists in every study, the possibility that the alternative hypothesis is statistically significant is reduced. If the noise factor is big it will overwhelm any observed differences between the means respectively representing the alternative and null hypotheses. The smaller the formula number the less likely it will "hurdle over" the table number and achieve the goal of significance (p.<.05) results. If the noise factor is small, the signal (the difference between alternative minus null) will have a greater chance of being statistically significant.

There is one final element in the basic interval/ratio level formula to discuss, sample size. The square root of sample size is divided into the standard deviation. This decreases the size of the noise indicator and therefore reduces noise's impact on the formula number. This is the main reason why researchers attempt to increase sample size. Larger samples usually have smaller variability than do smaller samples and therefore provide a bigger noise correction factor.

Figure 32 shows that the members of the family of interval/ratio inference test formulas have some slight differences from each other. In this primer the differences are discussed in the context of the formula similarities. These differences are emphasized in standard statistics textbooks, and they exist for several reasons. Both the Z test and the one group t test are used when we compare data from a single sample to data from the corresponding population. For example, you could have gathered a sample of IQ scores which is then compared to population IQ data (population data, as we learned earlier, is actually data from huge samples). Comparing the Z test and the one group t test formulas, we see that the only difference between the two formulas is the standard deviation symbol, σ or s. σ, or <u>little sigma</u>, is the symbol for the population standard deviation. It's presence in the Z test formula indicates that the formula can only be used when both the population mean <u>and</u> the population standard deviation are known. Researchers frequently do not have knowledge of both of these population parameters, and, of the two, it is the population standard deviation that is usually unknown. If it is unknown, then the population standard deviation is estimated, and replaced in the formula, by s, the sample standard deviation. The Z test then becomes the one group t test.

When the one group t test is compared to the two group dependent t test, several differences are noted. <u>First</u>, the two group dependent t test is used when two samples of data are compared. The two samples are dependent on each other; the data from samples are connected and can be compared on a case by case basis. <u>Second</u>, the single group sample mean, X bar, is replaced by D bar, which is the mean of the difference scores calculated by subtracting one set of scores from another. For example, an instructor gives a standardized exam to a group of students at the beginning of a term and then again at the end of the term. The instructor calculates a difference score for each student by subtracting the student's first score from the second one. Then the mean of the difference scores, D bar, is calculated by adding up all the difference scores and dividing by the number of students. The instructor's alternative hypothesis is that the scores on the second exam will be much higher than those on the first. This hypothesis is represented in the formula by D bar, and the bigger D bar is, the greater the overall difference is between the two sets of scores. In this example the null hypothesis is that there are no differences between the two sets of scores at the population level. Thus, the null hypothesis is represented by zero.

Sd is the symbol for the standard deviation of the difference scores. Once the instructor calculates the differences between the first and second set of scores, a standard deviation can be calculated from the set of difference scores. This standard deviation is the noise representative in the two group dependent t test formula.

When the two group dependent and independent t tests are compared, further differences emerge. In both tests two samples of data are compared. In the two group independent t test the two batches of sample data are not connected and therefore not comparable at the individual level. For example, the instructor gives a standardized exam at the end of the term to students in two separate classes which were exposed to different teaching techniques for the same material. Difference scores cannot be created because the two sets of scores do not come from the same individual (or are otherwise not directly comparable). The alternative hypothesis is represented by comparing the mean of one group of student scores, X bar one, to the mean of the other group of student scores, X bar two. In the formula the D bar is replaced by X bar one - X bar two. The greater the difference between the two sample means, then the greater the difference from the representative of the null hypothesis, zero. Zero represents the null again because the null hypothesis would predict that there will be no differences between the two populations represented by the two groups of scores.

Since a difference score based on each individual cannot be produced in the two group independent t test, a standard deviation of the difference scores also cannot be produced. Instead a variance (standard deviation squared) for <u>each</u> sample is produced. The noise factor in this formula takes into consideration the variability in each sample; S2 pooled is the combined variance for both samples. 1/N + 1/N is the sample size noise qualifier presented in a different manner. When the square root is taken, the denominator is at the same exponent level as the noise factor in all the other formulas.

The final causal interval/ratio inference test presented is called the F test. The F test is the inference test for a statistical technique known as <u>analysis of variance (Anova)</u>. In your introductory course you will most likely be confronted with Anova and the F test. The F test is logically connected to the other interval/ratio causal inference tests we just examined, and it is also based on the signal/noise inference test model shown in Figure 31. Examination of Figure 33 shows that the F test formula is, at first glance, different from the others. However, the F test is like the other interval/ratio tests, with a signal ("<u>between groups variance</u>") and a noise ("<u>within groups variance</u>") component. These terms are explained in Figure 33.

ANALYSIS OF VARIANCE: THE F TEST

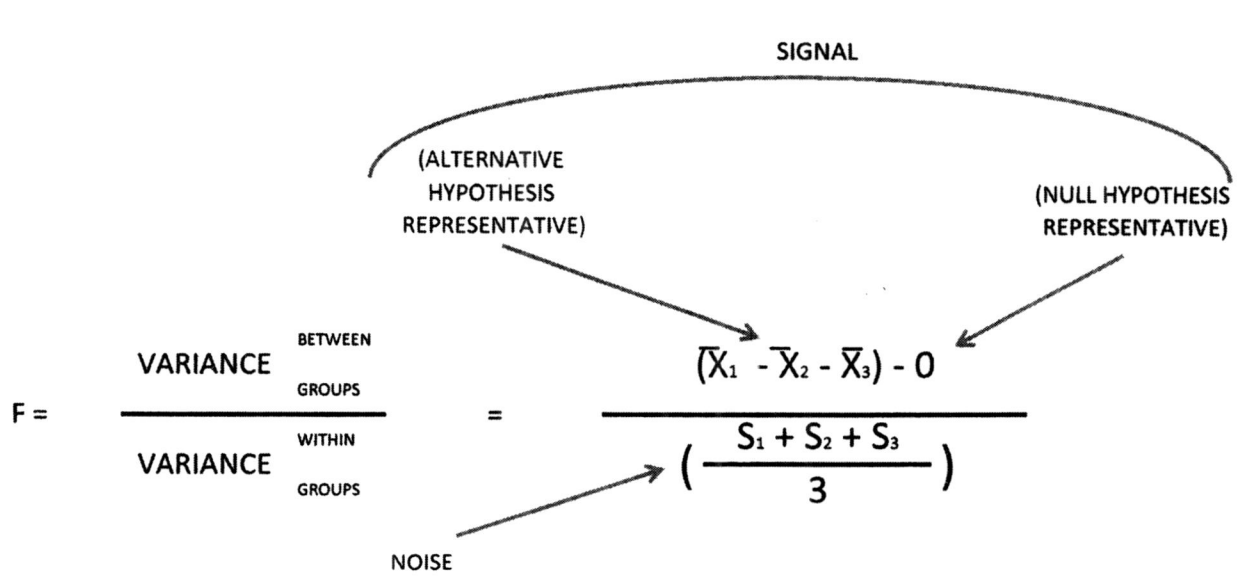

FIGURE 33

The F test is the interval/ratio inference test used when comparing 3 or more groups or conditions. Between groups variance has 3 or more sample means which are first compared to each other, then compared to zero. The sample means jointly represent the alternative hypothesis and zero represents the null hypothesis. Between groups variance is simply a convenient way to measure this overall difference between the sample means, and then between the overall difference and the population mean. A large overall difference between means, that is, between groups variance, indicates that at least one of the sample means is far apart from the others, and therefore far apart from zero.

Each sample mean comes from a distribution of scores that surrounds each mean. Within groups variance is an average of the variability of each group's distribution. The F test is just like the other interval/ratio tests, in that the numerator is composed of sample and population means, and the denominator, as the measure of noise, is composed of variances and sample sizes.

125

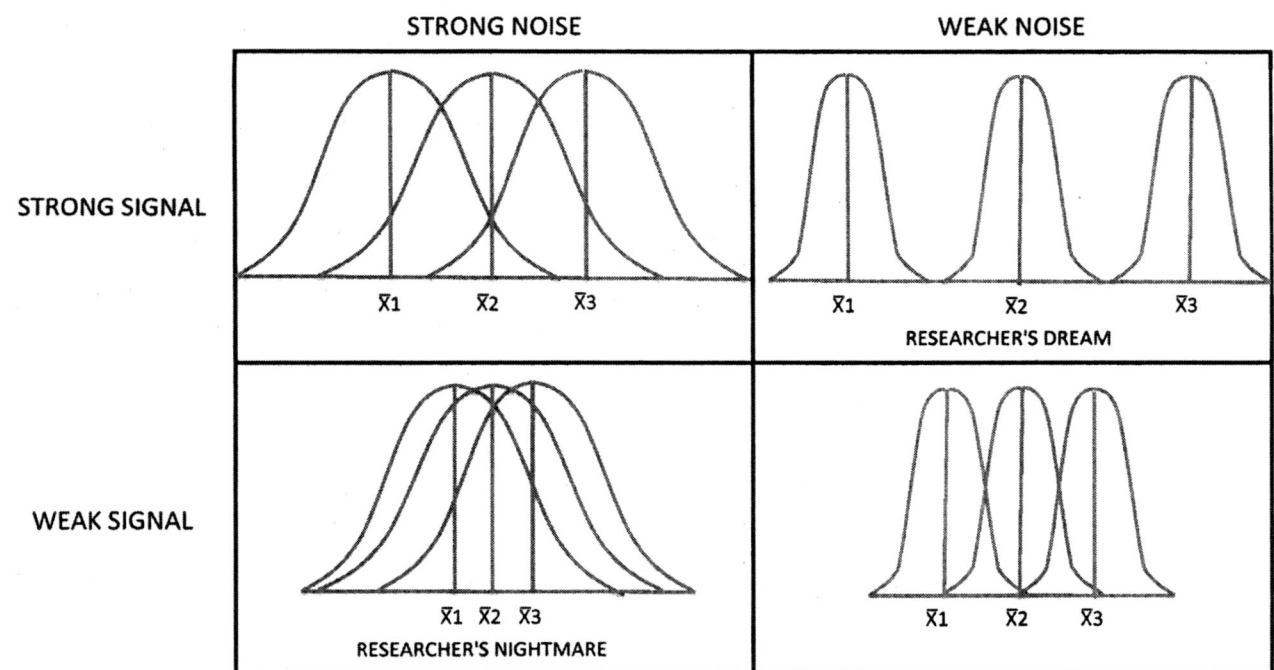

FIGURE 34

Perhaps this discussion of the F test can be enhanced by returning to a four cell signals/noise chart, introduced in Chapter 6. As before, Figure 34 is divided up into four cells, strong signal/strong noise, strong signal/weak noise, weak signal/strong noise, weak signal/weak noise. In each cell the signal is represented by the gap between the three sample means, and noise is represented by the three distribution curves moving away from the mean at the center of each distribution.

In the <u>strong signal/strong noise</u> cell the three means of the three respective distributions are far apart, indicating a strong signal. However, the three distributions are large and they somewhat overlap, indicating strong noise. Overlapping distributions means that a score in the overlapped area could have come from either of the overlapped distributions. The <u>weak signal/strong noise</u> cell is the worst possible outcome. Here the means are close together, indicating a weak signal. The signal is weak because three experimental groups that are treated differently should have large differences between their sample means. Noise remains strong, meaning that the three distributions are large and overlap. The strong signal/weak noise cell is the best possible outcome. In this cell the three means are far apart, indicating that the three differently treated groups reacted very differently. And, the distributions around each mean are quite small with no overlap. In the weak signal/weak noise cell, enough control was exerted to suppress variability. However the differential treatment of the three groups did not result in large sample mean differences.

D. Signals, noise and the correlation-regression family of interval/ratio inference tests.

Correlation and regression are related to ex post facto (after the fact) research, where researchers attempt to establish a linkage between two variables, but not a causal arrow. Since no attempt is being made to establish causality, the data are likely to have been gathered in a non-experimental research design without the use of independent variable manipulation or the use of random assignment. The interval/ratio level, like the other two levels, has its own correlation and regression formulas. The discussion of causality and correlation in Chapter 7 indicated that correlation is an attempt to ascertain whether two events are linked, by demonstrating that they are moving in the same direction (positive correlation) or in opposite directions (negative correlation). Even though finding that two events are correlated does not establish a causal relation between the events, correlation research can be used to test alternative hypotheses (two events are positively or negatively correlated) against the null hypothesis (two events are not correlated).

Figure 35 graphically demonstrates how this hypothesis testing is done. This is another signal/noise chart, divided into four quadrants or cells, strong signal/ strong noise, strong signal/weak noise, weak signal/strong noise, weak signal/ weak noise. The chart in each cell depicts a scatterplot, represented by the gray areas. The <u>scatterplot</u> is a graphical depiction of how each data point represents two numerical values from two different variables, for example, the height and the weight of a particular individual. This two-dimensional plot of points is analogous to the frequency distribution for one variable. It shows the relation between the variables: one is plotted on the X axis and the other on the Y axis. All the dots together create the "scatter."

The line drawn through the scatter is called the <u>line of best fit, or the regression line</u>. The line of best fit is analogous to a mean. The line goes through the scatter in such a way as to <u>one</u>, minimize the amount of scatter away from the line, and <u>two</u>, divide the scatter into two approximately equal groups above and below the line. As with the mean, the line of best fit represents the signal. The scatter off the line is considered noise. The more the scatter is dispersed from the line, the greater the noise or variability.

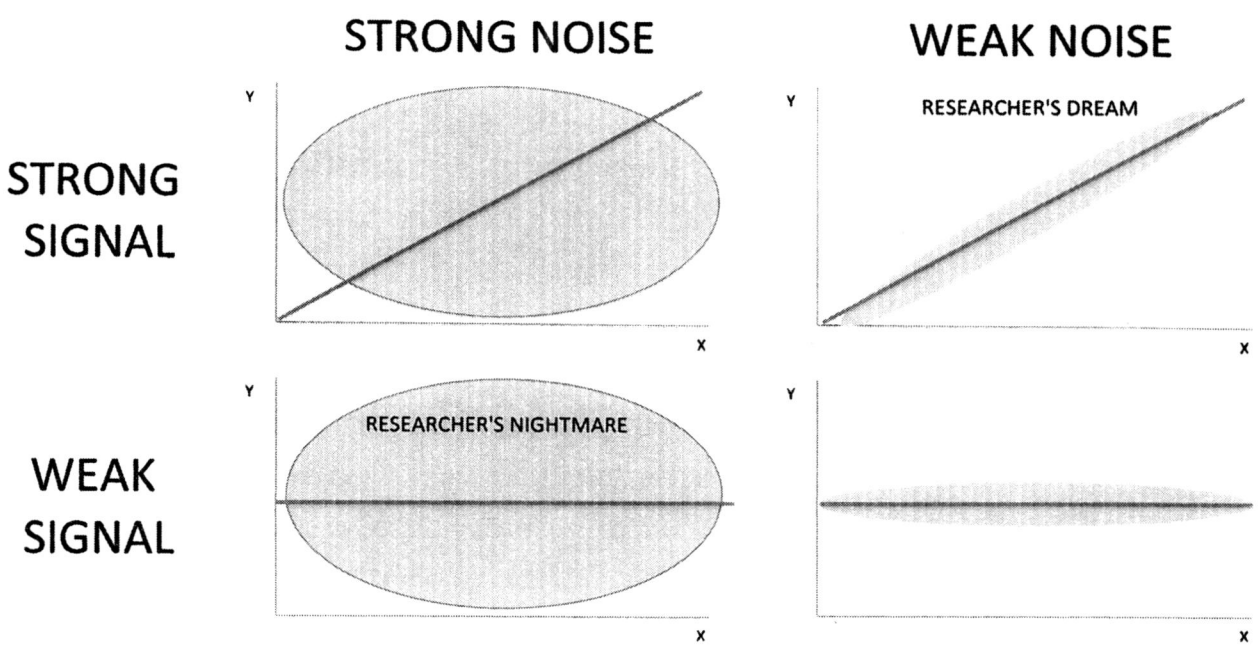

FIGURE 35

A sharply rising or falling line indicates a strong signal: the two variables are strongly co-related. If there is a no relation or a weak relation between the two variables, then the line remains basically flat or level.

In the <u>strong signal/weak noise</u> (researcher's dream cell) cell, the strong signal is indicated by a sharply rising (or falling) line of best fit. Weak noise is shown by the dots (the gray area) being close to the line. This cell could be indicative of the relation of the heights and weights of a sample of individuals of the same gender. Taller individuals usually weigh more than shorter individuals, and the range of weights for same-gender individuals of the same height is usually limited. In the <u>weak signal/strong noise</u> (researcher's nightmare) cell the line is level and the dots (the gray area) are scattered far and wide from the line. This cell indicates that there is no relation between the two variables, and that knowledge of one variable tells you nothing about the other variable. For example, the relation between height and intelligence could be indicated in this cell. Knowing a person's height will tell you nothing about his or her intelligence. For an individual of a given height, the corresponding IQ score could be anywhere on the intelligence continuum. In the <u>weak signal/weak noise</u> cell the situation is improved only slightly. There is no co-relation between the two variables. To use our previous example, there is a more limited range of possible IQ scores for individuals of any given height. In the <u>strong signal/strong noise</u> cell there is a positive correlation between the two variables with a wide but constantly rising range of scatter. For example, for individuals of a given height there is a wide range of possible weights, as might be the case if you were using a mixed gender sample.

At the interval/ratio level there are two correlational inference tests used to quantitatively measure the data graphically represented in a scatterplot. Figures 36 and 37 show these two tests: the <u>Pearson correlation coefficient</u> and the <u>t test for regression</u>. Both formulas have a signal numerator and a noise denominator.

As stated in Chapter 7, a researcher uses correlation to examine the strength of the relation between variables, without trying to establish which variable is the cause and which is the effect. The Pearson product moment correlation coefficient formula produces a descriptive statistic, and it is the interval/ratio level inference test used for correlation analysis.

INTERVAL/RATIO LEVEL CORRELATION TEST: THE PEARSON PRODUCT MOMENT CORRELATION COEFFICIENT

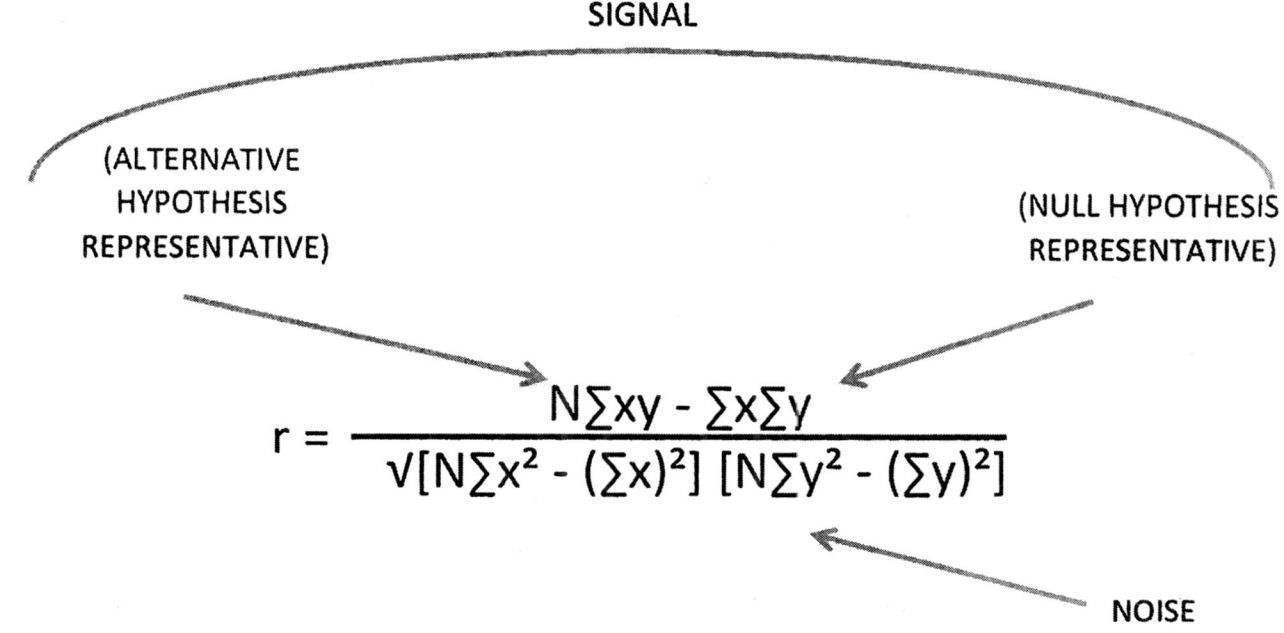

SIGNAL

(ALTERNATIVE HYPOTHESIS REPRESENTATIVE)

(NULL HYPOTHESIS REPRESENTATIVE)

$$r = \frac{N\sum xy - \sum x \sum y}{\sqrt{[N\sum x^2 - (\sum x)^2]\,[N\sum y^2 - (\sum y)^2]}}$$

NOISE

FIGURE 36

As a descriptive statistic the Pearson correlation coefficient measures the strength of association between two variables. A correlation coefficient is in a sense a descriptive statistic, analogous to a mean, in that it condenses a large amount of data into a single number, which ranges from +1.0 to -1.0. Since a normal distribution underlies each of the two variables compared, as shown in Figure 38, a correlation analysis is really comparing these two frequency distributions. The inference test purpose of the Pearson coefficient will be described after the discussion of regression analysis.

Regression analysis is a predictive, but not a causal analysis, falling somewhere between causal and correlational analyses. In regression an attempt is made to predict the values of one variable (e.g., height) from the values of another (e.g., birth length) using data that are gathered in a correlational, non-experimental manner.

THE INTERVAL/RATIO LEVEL REGRESSION TEST

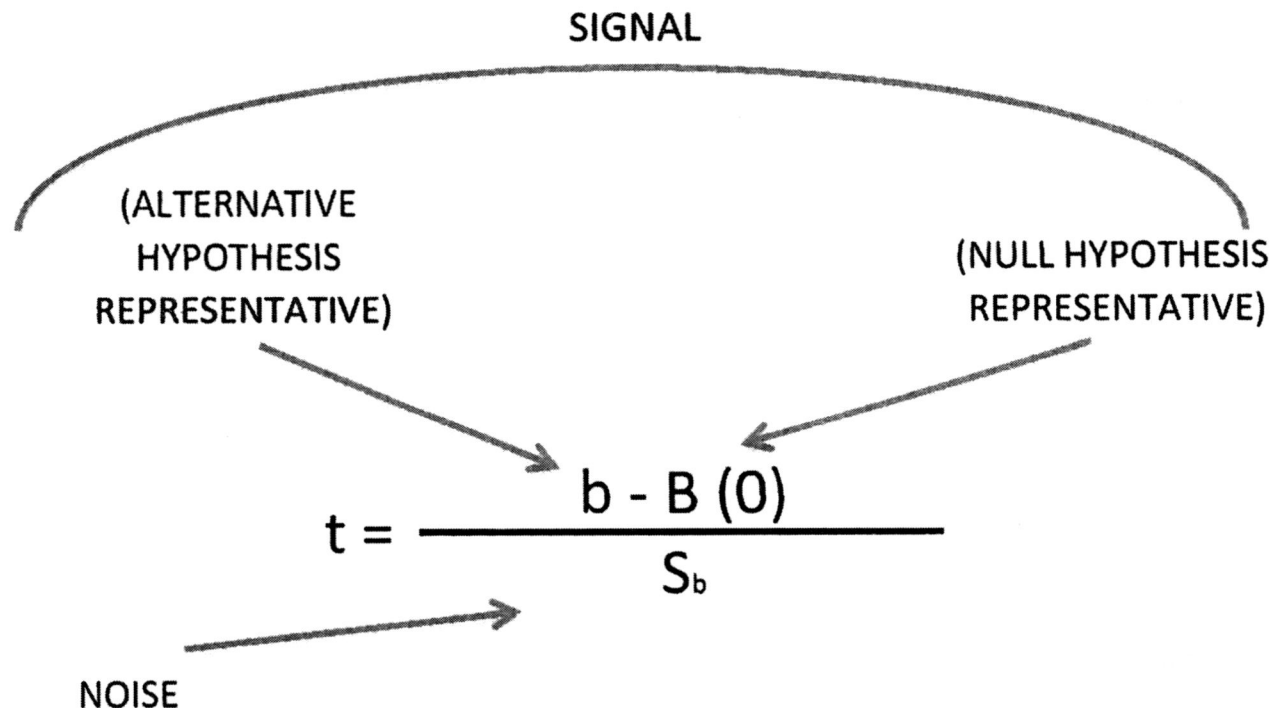

FIGURE 37

In the regression inference test (Figure 37) for simple regression (only one predictor variable) the signal is composed of b, the sample slope of the line of best fit representing the alternative hypothesis, minus B, the population slope of best fit, representing the null hypothesis. The null hypothesis assumes that B, the population slope, is zero, and therefore the line of best fit is flat. Noise is represented by Sb, the sample slope standard error. What is standard error? It is a measure of the amount of variability that would be present among different slopes estimated from samples drawn from the same population. Another way of saying it is that the standard error is the standard deviation of the sampling distribution of b's.

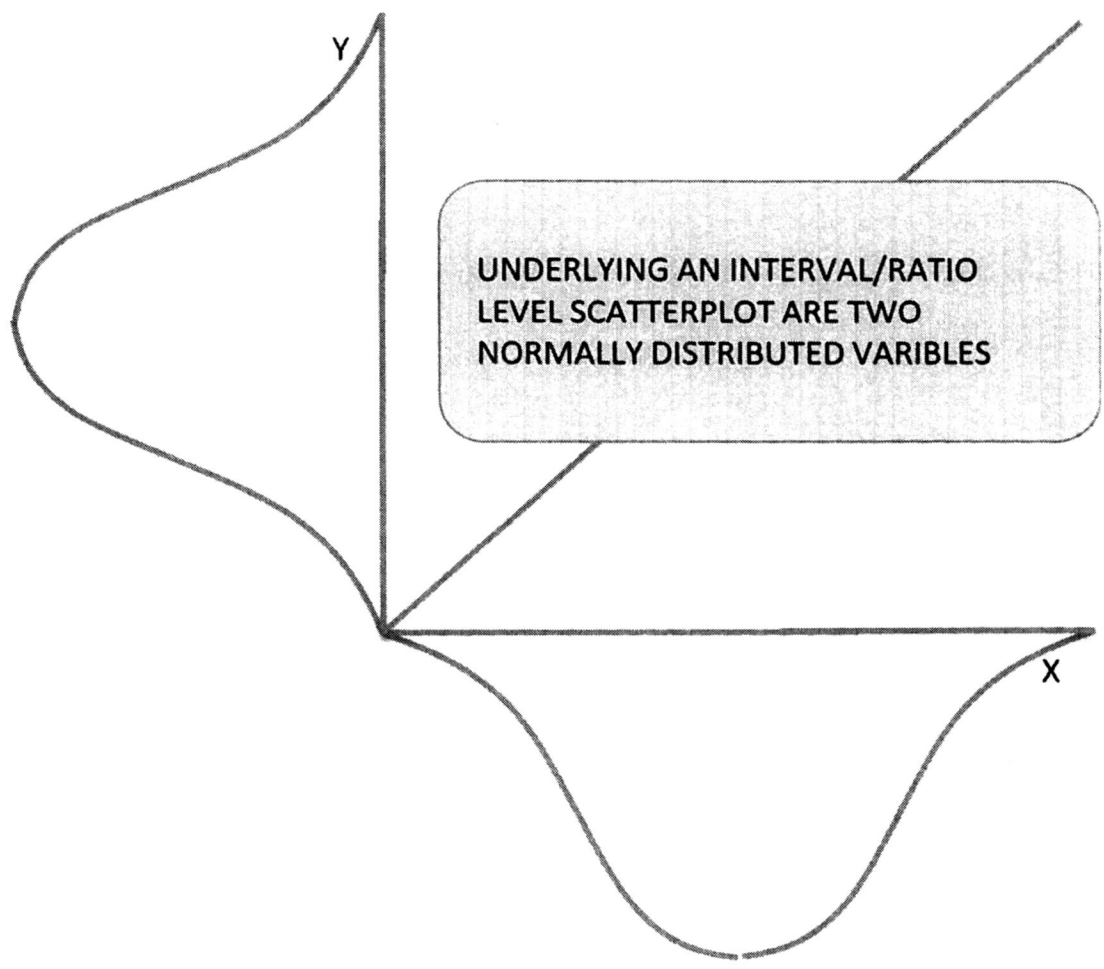

FIGURE 38

The greater the difference between the sample and population slope, the stronger the signal. A formula number is derived when the signal is divided by the noise, and the formula number is compared to the appropriate number in the t table (or F tables, if there is more than one predictor variable, as in multiple regression), as indicated in the six step processing model.

Why are the t and F statistics used as the inference tests in regression? The regression analysis discussed here is in the interval/ratio inference test family. It is based on metric, continuous data and the normal distribution. Simple linear regression, where the values of one variable are predicted from the values of just one other variable, is analogous to t tests, where two (and only two) means are being compared. This is the form of the interval/ratio regression inference test that is demonstrated in Figure 37. Multiple linear regression, where the values of one variable are predicted from the values of two or more other variables, is analogous to an ANOVA, where more than two means are being compared. Thus the F statistic is appropriate for testing a multiple regression model which has at least two predictor variables.

Now we can return to the second purpose of the Pearson correlation coefficient formula (Figure 36). In the formula, the alternative hypothesis representative sums the multiplicative product of each data point. For example, if the X variable is height and the Y variable is weight, then the height and weight of each individual is multiplied, and then all these multiplied products are summed. This operation assumes that the correlation of the two variables affects each possible interaction of the two variables. The null hypothesis, that there is no co-relation between the variables, does not first multiply each x and y data point values. In this case all the heights and weights are first separately summed, and then the two summations are multiplied. This operation assumes that there is no interaction between the X and Y variables that affects each interaction; in other words, there is no correlation.

The denominator or noise portion of the formula looks complicated, but in essence it is a way of measuring the variability within the range of scores in each variable (X and Y).

The correlation coefficient that is the product of the formulas shown in Figure 36 measures the degree to which the regression analysis produces accurate predictions. Since the line of best fit produced by the regression analysis will realistically not account for all data points in the scatter, we need some measure of how well the line accurately maps the data. If there was a perfect fit between scores on one variable with the scores on the other variable (which never occurs in actual research) then all dots in the scatter will be on the line. In this case there is no noise, and the Pearson correlation coefficient will equal +1.0 (positive correlation) or -1.0 (negative correlation). The sign of r is the same as that of the sample regression coefficient, b, and indicates the direction of the slope. When the correlation coefficient is close to 0, most of the dots are not on the regression line; they are scattered away from the line. A correlation coefficient of zero means the absence of a relation between the two variables, and the regression line of best fit will be completely level.

E. A useful application of the normal curve concept

Before leaving the discussion of interval/ratio inference tests, let's return to the normal distribution one more time. Measurement experts have found a way to use the normal distribution logic on data collected from parametric variables that are badly skewed from normal, and even on data collected at nonparametric (nominal and ordinal) levels!

Since data are always collected from samples we never know about any of the parameters of a population, including the population distribution. However, if we collect data on a continuous variable, we can reasonably assume that the population underlying the sample data is normally distributed.

If the assumption of a normal population distribution cannot be made, we can assume that something known as the sampling distribution of the mean is normally distributed. If this assumption can be made, then the parametric sample-to-population inference process based on the normal distribution can be used even if the specific sample is not normally distributed.

The central limit theorem is a mathematical theorem specifying the theoretical characteristics of the normal distribution. It states that, for continuous, quantitative variables the sampling distribution of sample means will be normally distributed even if the actual samples leading to each mean are not normally distributed. What is the sampling distribution of the mean?

A sampling distribution is a theoretical probability distribution of the possible values of some sample statistic that would occur if one were to draw all possible samples of this statistic of a fixed size from a given population. If one were to take an infinite number of samples from a population, one could derive an infinite number of sample means. This set of sample means would have a distribution, known as the sampling distribution of the mean. According to the central limit theorem, the sampling distribution of means will have a normal distribution, and the mean of the distribution would be the population mean. A sampling distribution of a statistic is always theoretical because no one would ever take the time to draw and do research on all possible samples from a population. It just so happens, as will be demonstrated in the example below, that a sampling distribution of a statistic tends to be normal (if the number of samples is sufficiently large), even if the raw value samples, and even the population, are not normal.

You are a statistics instructor with a class of 40 students. You ask each student to put their height, rounded off to the nearest inch, on a small slip of paper. You collect the slips, wad them up, and put them all in a wide mouth jar. You shake the jar vigorously and draw out ten of the slips. You have your students plot the frequency distribution of that particular sample and calculate the mean of that sample. You then replace the ten slips in the jar and shake vigorously again. You then take out a second sample of ten heights. Again you have your students plot the distribution and calculate the sample mean. You repeat this process 20 times. Then you have your students calculate a grand mean of all 20 sample means, and plot a distribution of the 20 sample means.

What will your students discover from this process? First, none of the samples will be perfectly normal in their distributions, and some of the samples will have very non-normal distributions. It is likely that the distribution of sample means around the grand mean will have a more normal distribution than any of the individual samples. Although the sampling distribution of means is centered on the population mean, any one estimate of the population mean will differ from the population mean; hence, a measure of the variability of the individual sample mean estimates around the population mean is needed. What is needed is the standard deviation of the sample means in the sampling distribution. This is known as the standard error.

An extension of this example shows that the sampling distribution of the means is more normal than the population distribution. Using your class as the population, you ask your students to create a population distribution from all 40 heights and to find the population mean. You then have them compare the population distribution to the distribution of sample means. The population mean should be identical to the grand mean of sample means, and the shape of the sample means distribution curve should be more normal than that of the population.

This example demonstrates that statistics derived from interval/ratio data, in this case means, are more normally distributed than the raw values generated in each sample. This empirical demonstration of the central limit theorem could be done with any continuous, quantitative data.

The concept of the theoretical sampling distribution of a statistic allows for the use of the normal curve as a frame of reference against which to evaluate a single sample descriptive statistic, such as a sample mean. Through comparison with the theoretical normal sampling distribution of means, the placement of that sample mean under the curve can be labeled as common, unusual, or rare. If we find that the occurrence of an event is rare, we can conclude that non-chance factors (the alternative hypothesis) caused this rare outcome. The null hypothesis of no difference can be rejected, and the alternative hypothesis of a difference can be accepted.

This discussion of the theoretical sampling distribution of means leads to a fundamental, and often confusing, point about nonparametric statistics. <u>The random sampling distribution of many nonparametric (nominal and ordinal) statistics approximates a normal distribution when the sample size is greater than 25</u>, even if the underlying population distribution is not normal. This means that parametric inference tests can often be used on data gathered at nonparametric measurement levels if the sample size is greater than 25. This is a reason why nonparametric inference tests are under-discussed in introductory texts.

Parametric inference tests based on infinitely quantifiable data from continuums are more statistically powerful than nonparametric inference tests. <u>Statistical</u> <u>power</u>, first discussed in Chapter 5, is the ability to reject the null hypothesis when in fact the null hypothesis is false at the population level. Statistical power can vary, and one of the factors that cause this variation is level of measurement. For example, the t test inference formula, which is based on an interval level of measurement, has greater statistical power than a sign test, which is based on the ordinal level of measurement. Why is this so? The sign test, like all ordinal level based tests, does not use the specific information leading to a more or less quantitative judgment.

You have asked a group of respondents to indicate which of two brands of jeans they like better, by having them rate each brand using the same 10 point rating scale. If a respondent liked brand X better than brand Y, you give that respondent a plus, and if a respondent liked Y better than X, you give the respondent a minus. You then compare the number of pluses and minuses in the sign test formula. However, you could have used a t test on this data, since the rating scale is at the interval level of measurement. You could have created a difference score for each respondent, comparing each person's rating for Brand X with the rating for Brand Y. Instead of a crude, nonspecific plus or minus measure of intensity, you now have a calibrated interval scale of intensity across 10 categories. Unlike the sign test, the t test uses this specific intensity information, and because it does you are more likely to get a statistically significant result, than if you had used the sign test.

Section 3:

Conclusion

I have discussed the seven basic concepts of statistics in Section 1 and I have demonstrated how these concepts are integrated into the most prominent inference test formulas in Section 2. Section 3 has two chapters. In Chapter 11 a statistical decision tree is presented. The purpose of this decision tree is to demonstrate how researchers decide which inference test to use for a particular data analysis. Chapter 12 presents final thoughts and further references to enhance your understanding of inferential statistics.

Chapter 11:

The statistical decision tree

Chapter 11 presents a decision tree applied to statistics. The statistical decision tree will help you to accurately and quickly assess which inference test is best for the sample data collected. Once this assessment is made, the statistical software can be programmed to calculate the probability of the event of interest via the selected inference test and the six step processing model. Ultimately all learning in statistics is geared to correctly answering the questions incorporated into the decision tree.

As each specific question in the tree is presented, hopefully you will see that your knowledge of the seven basic concepts presented in this book will be useful in selecting the appropriate inference test.

Why do you need to know when to use a particular inference test? Although most organizations only use descriptive statistics in their numerical decision making, increased computational power is slowly expanding the use of inferential statistics. The increasing use of inferential statistics means that many professionals need to understand enough research design and statistical concepts to know <u>when</u> a particular inference test should be used in order to be a competent professional.

A. The logic of the decision tree.

Most software menus are decision trees. When you turn on a computer the first screen is usually a main menu. This menu indicates the programs or software packages that are installed in the computer. You indicate to the computer which program you wish to access. When you are in that particular program, you indicate which part of the program you wish to access. Each choice takes you to a more specific level of the program. This is a decision tree in action. In a decision tree you start with the most general question or choice. Each of the succeeding levels is more specific than the one before it. The statistical inference test decision tree exactly follows this logic.

B. The decision tree, step by step.

Figures 39 and 40 demonstrate the quesitons and answers in the statistical decision tree. The <u>first</u> question is: Describe a single sample or infer from

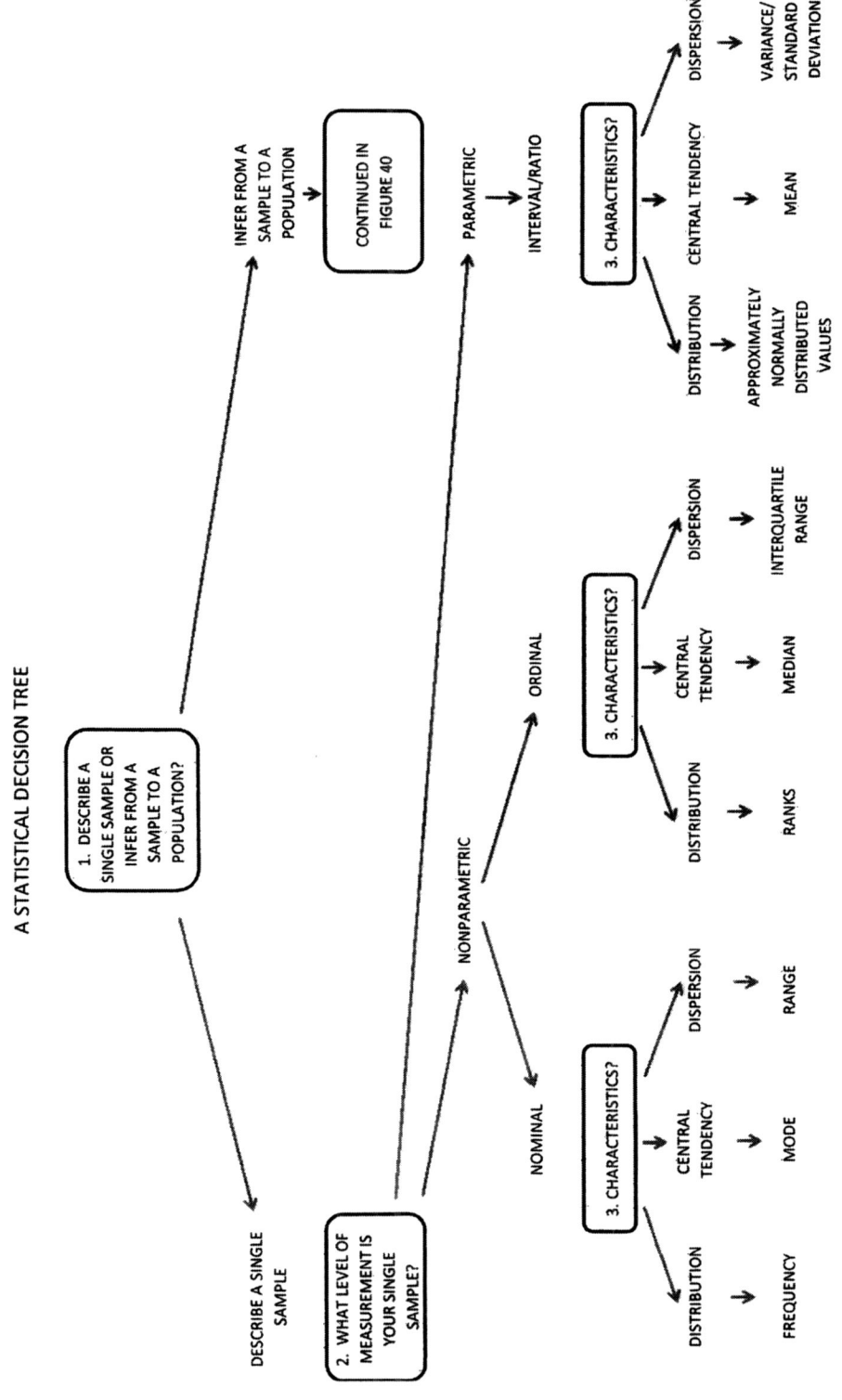

FIGURE 39

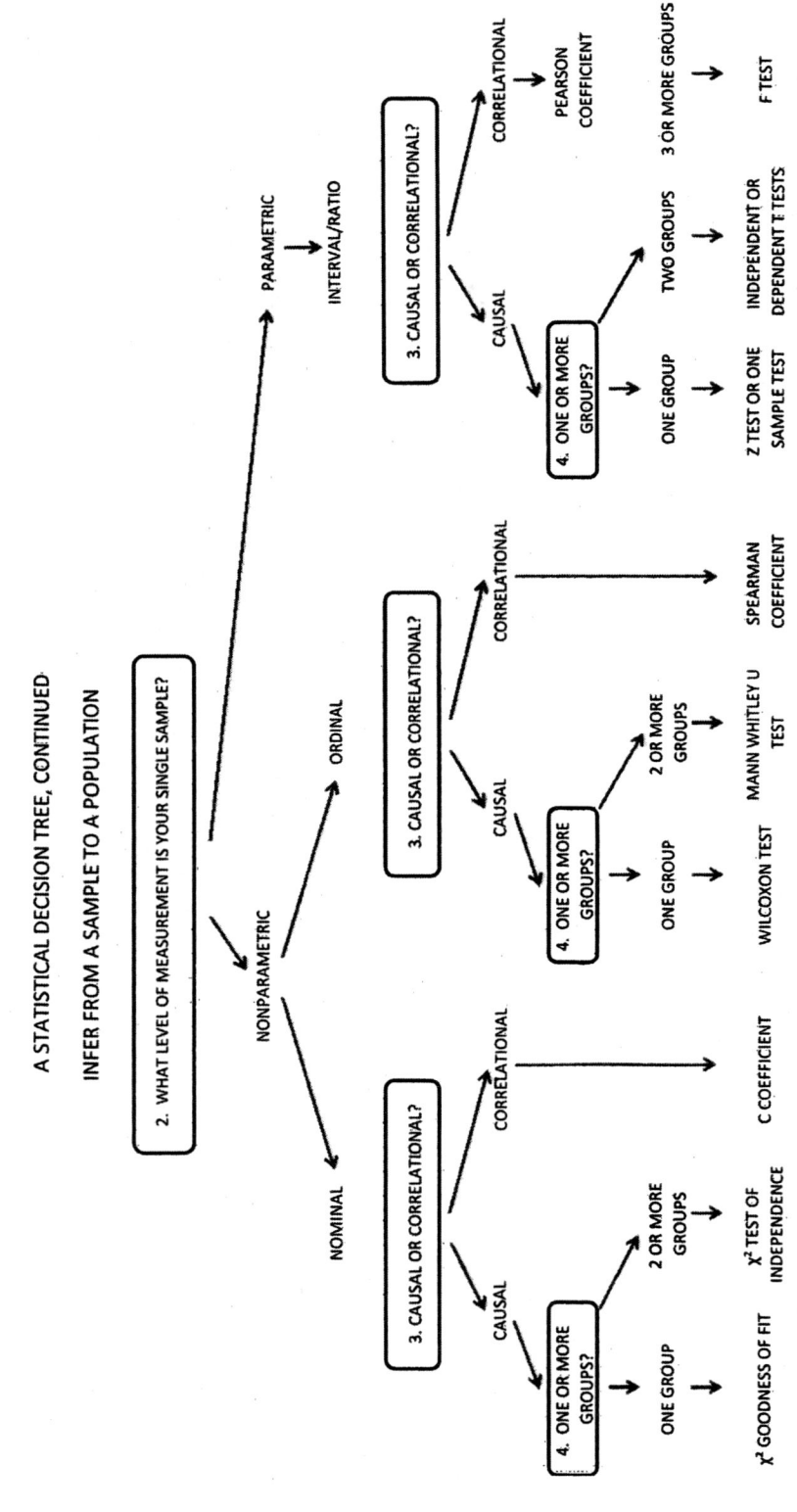

A STATISTICAL DECISION TREE, CONTINUED

INFER FROM A SAMPLE TO A POPULATION

2. WHAT LEVEL OF MEASUREMENT IS YOUR SINGLE SAMPLE?

PARAMETRIC

INTERVAL/RATIO

3. CAUSAL OR CORRELATIONAL?

CORRELATIONAL → PEARSON COEFFICIENT

CAUSAL

4. ONE OR MORE GROUPS?

ONE GROUP → Z TEST OR ONE SAMPLE TEST

TWO GROUPS → INDEPENDENT OR DEPENDENT t TESTS

3 OR MORE GROUPS → F TEST

NONPARAMETRIC

ORDINAL

3. CAUSAL OR CORRELATIONAL?

CORRELATIONAL → SPEARMAN COEFFICIENT

CAUSAL

4. ONE OR MORE GROUPS?

ONE GROUP → WILCOXON TEST

2 OR MORE GROUPS → MANN WHITLEY U TEST

NOMINAL

3. CAUSAL OR CORRELATIONAL?

CORRELATIONAL → C COEFFICIENT

CAUSAL

4. ONE OR MORE GROUPS?

ONE GROUP → χ^2 GOODNESS OF FIT

2 OR MORE GROUPS → χ^2 TEST OF INDEPENDENCE

FIGURE 40

a sample or samples to a population? Answering this question takes you to descriptive (describing single samples) or inferential (inferring from samples to populations) statistics. If you answered "infer from a sample to a population", the <u>second</u> question is: What is the level of measurement in your sample? The answer has two components. First you must decide whether the data are nonparametric or parametric. If the answer is nonparametric, you must then decide if you have nominal or ordinal data. All parametric data are interval/ratio. The <u>third</u> question varies depending on your answer to question 1: descriptive or inferential statistics. In descriptive statistics the third question is: What characteristics (i.e., distribution, central tendency, dispersion) of the sample do you wish to describe? The actual statistic calculated follows from the particular characteristic chosen. On the inferential side the third question is: Is the inferred relation causal or correlational? The correlational answer leads directly to the particular inference tests to be used. The causal answer leads to one <u>final</u> question: How many groups or variable conditions are in the study? The particular inference test used varies with group or condition number.

As an example of how a researcher would use the decision tree, let's again use basketball sales in different seasons of the year. The researcher's response to the first question (Describe a single sample or infer from sample data to a population?) is that you wish to infer from sample data to a population. The response to the second question (What level of measurement is your sample?) is nonparametric, and more specifically, nominal. The third question asks whether the analysis is to be causal or correlational, and in this example the answer is causal. Since you are only interested in the sale of basketballs in one store in one calendar year, the answer to the final question (One or more groups or conditions?) is just one condition. Therefore the selected inference test is the chi square goodness of fit test.

Once you know the particular inference test you need to properly analyze your data, then you simply program your statistical software to perform the necessary computations for that particular test. Although each of the commercially available statistical software programs has its own idiosyncrasies regarding the actual programming steps, these programs all attempt to achieve the same goal, which is to process the data according to the six step processing model. Any of the programs will initiate the processing model, starting at step 2. If you have asked your program to run an inference test, the printout of the test will show you the desired final outcome, the probability statement. Usually the printout will show you some other information, such as the name of the test, the sample size or sizes the test utilized, the descriptive statistics utilized, and some of the numbers and calculations that were part of the test.

In the basketball sales and seasons example, most statistical programs will provide you with the following information. The printout indicates that you selected the chi square goodness of fit test, the names of the two variables being compared (basketball sales and seasons), the observed and expected frequencies for the comparison in each of the four seasons, the number of degrees of freedom, the chi square formula number, and the probability statement.

Chapter Summary

A statistical inference test decision tree is a crucial bridge between data collection and data analysis. Once data are collected researchers can answer the four questions in the tree to determine which data analyses (specifically, which inference tests) are appropriate.

Chapter 12:

Other Resources for the Statistically Stressed

You may have reached the end of this primer saying to yourself: I still don't understand inferential statistics! Or you may find that your understanding is fragmentary. Perhaps your understanding is illusive, in the sense that one day you think you understand a concept and then the next day you don't! If this might be you, don't give up in despair quite yet! Many students have these reactions to their first exposure to inferential statistics.

There is no denying that inferential statistics is a complex topic based on a way of thinking that is foreign to many people. Given this alien complexity, if you were to set aside this primer of a few months and then read it again, you might be surprised by how much your understanding has increased. Or, if you were to read some of the references listed below, and then read the primer again, your understanding may increase dramatically.

For many people a solid understanding of inferential statistics can take years, requiring periodic exposure to statistics through books, courses, and research and data analysis experience. If your exposure to and experience with inferential statistics increases over time, you will find that your understanding broadens and deepens. Your understanding will broaden because you will be exposed to a wider variety of inference tests, or to a wider variety of uses for the tests you already know. Your understanding will also deepen because you will be able to more fully connect symbols, inference test formulas, and the concepts presented in this primer. You might want to keep this primer because re-reading it periodically as you use inferential statistics will deepen your understanding by further emphasizing the connection of statistics to the underlying concepts.

I have tried to simplify statistics by presenting underlying concepts. Other authors have taken different approaches to simplifying statistics. You may benefit from exposure to some of these approaches. None of the references presented and discussed below are traditional introductory statistics textbooks.

Even though it is now over fifty years old, you may find Darrell Huff's classic How to Lie with Statistics (1954; W.W. Norton) still useful. This book is still in print, which means people are still buying it! This book is especially good at showing how simple, descriptive statistics can be subtly altered to fit the preconceptions of the user.

For those of you with very high levels of math anxiety, I recommend Mind Over Math by Kogelman and Warren (1978; McGraw-Hill). This book first discusses the psychology of math anxiety and the myths that people have about mathematics. The latter part of the book is devoted to a very gentle, simplified approach of formulas, algebra, and even calculus.

For gentler, kinder approaches to probability and inferential statistics, I recommend three books. Probability Without Tears: A Primer for Non-mathematicians by Derek Rowntree (1994; McMillan) covers many of the probability topics covered in standard statistical textbooks, but in a simpler, easier to understand fashion. Similarly, <u>Statistics Without Tears, A Primer for Non-mathematicians</u> by Rowntree (2003; Allyn and Bacon) provides simplified discussions of the connection between probability and inferential statistics. <u>Beating Murphy's Law, the Amazing Science of Risk</u>, by Bob Berger (1994; Dell) is even more user friendly to the non-mathematician. This book explains probability in words, pictures and examples, using very few numbers, and without using formulas.

Three other books give somewhat nontraditional approaches to inferential statistics, including probability. Gonick and Smith's <u>Cartoon Guide to Statistics</u> (1993, Harper Collins) presents the topics of inferential statistics in a traditional sequence, but the cartoon illustrations used throughout the book can be very helpful in illuminating statistical concepts. Kranzler, Kranzler and Moursund's <u>Statistics for the Terrified</u> (2003, Prentice Hall) is essentially a pared down statistics textbook that presents some statistical concepts and formulas in a very simplified fashion. Finally, the "Dummies" series has at last gotten around to statistics. Statistics for Dummies by Deborah Rumsey (2003, Wiley) also discusses inferential statistics in a simplified fashion.

There are many other books that also attempt to present statistical topics in simplified, easier to understand formats. My purpose here is not to present an exhaustive reference list, but to let you know that help is available! Remember, a nonmathematical person can understand and learn to use inferential statistics, so don't give up!

CPSIA information can be obtained at www.ICGtesting.com
Printed in the USA
BVOW06s0050210415

396996BV00004B/55/P